BADMINTON

BADMINTON

E. BROWN

FABER AND FABER
3 Queen Square
London

First published in 1969
This edition published 1975
by Faber and Faber Limited
3 Queen Square London WC1
Printed in Great Britain by
Whitstable Litho Ltd., Whitstable, Kent
All rights reserved

ISBN 0 571 10659 5 (Faber Paper Backs)
ISBN 0 571 08795 7 (hard bound edition)

CONTENTS

ILLUSTRATIONS

FIGURES

millimetres	mm or in	inches
25·4	1	0·04
50·8	2	0·08
76·2	3	0·12
101·6	4	0·16
127·0	5	0·20
152·4	6	0·24
177·8	7	0·28
203·2	8	0·32
228·6	9	0·35
254·0	10	0·39
508·0	20	0·79
762·0	30	1·18
1016	40	1·58
1270	50	1·97
1524	60	2·36
1778	70	2·76
2032	80	3·15
2286	90	3·54
2540	100	3·94

ACKNOWLEDGEMENTS

A KNOWLEDGE of badminton does not grow overnight, nor is it developed in isolation. I have had many mentors to whom I am deeply grateful; it would be invidious, although tempting, to select any names for special mention. The book required much preparation and I would particularly like to thank Rosamund Bartlett and Judith Short for their help and my wife for her moral and physical sustenance.

I would also like to thank the International Badminton Federation for permission to include their Laws (Appendix II), and Mr. Ray Williams for permission to quote from his paper on circuit training which was distributed to national badminton coaches.

INTRODUCTION

THIS BOOK HAS been written in the hope that it will help more people to enjoy playing badminton.

Badminton has many attractions. It is easy to play, indeed there can be few games that are easier. Even people new to the game can be seen enjoying quite long rallies and using a variety of strokes. Thus most of the exercise is gained from hitting the shuttle, and not from picking it up off the floor. But it also presents a challenge. Most players find no difficulty in improving, up to a certain standard, and there is a challenge in reaching that standard. To climb beyond this plateau presents a further challenge, a challenge that may be accepted only if one is willing to work. To practise. To concentrate. To strive.

The game itself is intrinsically attractive. The variety of pace, length and angle of shots is immense. The shuttle has been timed at about 100 mph off the rackets of top-class players. Seconds later the same players may be caressing the shuttle over the net so that it falls gently and slowly. There is a place in the game for the player who loves a ding-dong battle, but his antithesis, who wins by art and craft, has ample scope.

It is a social game. Doubles is the most usual game played in clubs. Those waiting to play are often close enough to the court to enjoy the game and, even if club custom encourages it, to comment audibly on the play or players.

There is plenty of competitive play. The number of tournaments seems to become greater every year. The entries in most continue to rise. Leagues are available for most clubs to join; a level of competition may usually be found to meet the ambitions of most clubs. Friendly matches between neighbouring clubs abound. Most clubs have their own tournaments, restricted to their own members. One of the great problems is the lack of suitable halls. Despite this, the game flourishes and spreads.

This book then is written about a most enjoyable game. I have tried to avoid repetition, not only because this would make the book bulky, but also because it can be very boring. This means, however, that some points may be missed if only selected chapters are read. To make best use of this book, I would suggest the reader skim through it to get an idea of its contents, and then read again more carefully, those points relevant to his needs. It is hoped that it will encourage those who have never tried it to have a go; help those who are beginners to get to know the game quickly; provide experienced players with a basis for critical examination of their game; and give teachers and potential coaches a basic understanding of the game on which to build their instruction. But above all, it is written in the hope that it will tempt more people to leave their homes to enjoy badminton, a warm game to play on a cold winter evening.

1

THE GAME

THIS CHAPTER DEALS with the court, the object of the game, the rules, equipment and other prerequisites of good badminton.

Court

Figure 1 is a plan view on which the correct dimensions have been marked. The net is 5 ft. high at the centre (5 ft. 1 in. at the posts at the side of the court). In doubles the whole court is used; the singles court is narrower. You will see that the service courts for doubles and singles are also different sizes. The court needs to be in a hall with a ceiling at least 25 ft. high if a satisfying game is to be played.

Object

The object of the game is to win by hitting the shuttle onto the floor within your opponent's court or by forcing him to hit it into the net or out of court on his own or your side of the net. Obviously if you can strike the shuttle above and close to the net your chances of winning the point are high. The further back you are from the net the more time your opponent has to see and play the shuttle. Thus much of the strategy of the game is to create situations in which your opponent will be forced to make a short return. When this situation does arise the rally should be finished, shortly and sharply. But you'll never do this if you are not in the right position. This is the reason for the insistence throughout this book on moving into the shuttle to

1 The Badminton court

play it close to the net and hit it while it is still well above net level. Hence also the emphasis on overhead shots.

Most players develop to some extent the knack of timing the hitting of the shuttle to obtain maximum speed with the minimum of effort. In achieving this they also develop the strength and flexibility of their wrist. The game demands that the reflexes become quicker and also that the movements about the court become faster but more controlled. Because rallies are fairly easy to play there is ample opportunity to develop one's ability quickly and, with experience, tactical skill also develops. But strokes, reflexes, movements and tactical skill are all interdependent, hence they *all* need to be developed. It is pointless to argue which is the most important. But it is significant that most players will consciously try to develop their strokes and tactics, but leave their reflexes and movements entirely to chance.

Laws

The laws of badminton are in Appendix II. They are short and fairly simple and well worth the effort of at least one reading. No one expects players to have a detailed knowledge of the Laws, such as is possessed by an umpire, but there is no excuse for the player who causes ill-feeling by his ignorance of them.

Shuttles

You will see from the laws that shuttles should weigh from 73 to 85 grains, should have 14 to 16 feathers fixed in a cork base 1 to $1\frac{1}{8}$ in. in diameter. The length and spread of the feathers is also specified. This specification is designed to ensure that, within certain limits, all shuttles will behave in a similar way. The variation in weight is to provide for variations in atmospheric conditions within halls. Since there are variations there must be a method of deciding which shuttle to use under which conditions. The Laws say that it is the correct pace 'if, when a player of average strength strikes it with a full underhand stroke from a spot immediately above one back boundary line in a line parallel to the side lines, and at an upward. angle, it falls not less than 1 ft., and not more than 2 ft. 6 in. short of the other back boundary line'.

Many clubs I have visited use shuttles that are too slow, and this has two adverse effects. Since club players are not usually of a very high standard, they find it impossible to play the shuttle to a length, or to play really effective smashes. Ladies in particular have difficulty in making the shuttle travel far and fast: the consequence is an indifferent game in which the defence is usually in command. The club players become used to this play and are reluctant to change, despite the Laws. The other adverse effect is seen in the club accounts. In an attempt to generate pace the players hit the shuttle harder and harder. Now, unless you are a good player, the harder you try to hit the shuttle, the more likely you are to mistime it. Mis-hitting not only damages the shuttle, it also damages the racket strings, thus leading to a double expense. It would be ridiculous to suggest that using the correct speed of shuttle will immediately improve the quality of the game and decrease the expenses; this will come slowly because old habits die hard. But it does mean that players should find that they can play a wider variety of shots more easily which should lead to increased variety in their game.

In each box of 'feathers' there is a note about storage, which everyone who has care of shuttles should 'read, mark, learn and inwardly digest'. The same kind of care needs to be taken on court. Be careful, when picking up the shuttle, not to bend the vanes of the feathers the wrong way: this is one of the finest methods of reducing its life span. If the vanes do get bent, straighten them quickly before you serve. Pick up the shuttle between rallies and play it or hand it to the server; it doesn't like to be scuffed along the floor. Take care to hit it cleanly in play even if you have to sacrifice a little pace, and you will find not only that your mistakes are reduced but also that the pace you have sacrificed is gradually recovered.

The Laws also permit 'the use of modified shuttles (e.g.

plastic, nylon, etc.)'. I do not suppose that there ever will be agreement on the 'plastic *v.* feather' question. There is, however, little doubt that the latest nylon shuttles are a tremendous improvement on those produced several years ago, and there are not many reasons why a badminton club that is having a difficult time financially because of the cost of 'feathers' should not change to nylon. There are qualifications of course. If the club plays in matches and there is no league available in which plastic/nylon shuttles are used, it may have little alternative to continuing with 'feathers'. Similarly if its members are interested in tournament play, it may not be practical to make the change. There are different speeds of plastic/nylon shuttles. There are different makes, having slightly different characteristics. Don't hesitate to experiment with them; they can provide just as enjoyable a game as a 'feather'.

Rackets

A very wide variety of rackets is available at a wide variety of prices—something to suit all pockets. But of course there are rackets and rackets. If you can afford a good quality one, buy it. And with one exception which I will mention later, buy one strung with gut. If you buy your racket at the beginning of the season, make sure that it is not one of last year's models, because gut does deteriorate and the dry summer months can take much of the life out of it. I do not know of any scientific tests that may have been made to differentiate one make from another, therefore I can give you no advice on this score. But there is no doubt that some shops and makers have a better reputation for their 'after-sales service', and it is worth seeking advice from any experienced players you may know.

If you are buying a racket for the first time you may find the following general comments helpful. The weight should be about 5 oz. It should have a thin flexible shaft and a slim frame made of several layers of wood glued together. The handle should be small enough to allow you to wrap your last three fingers round it so that they touch, or almost touch, the palm.

The balance should be about even. The grip should be comfortable and should tend towards square; it should never be round. Have a look at a few expensive rackets to get some idea of the appearance.

The racket you buy will be strung with either gut or nylon. Both should be thin: again look at the good quality rackets. The gut has the advantage of being more evenly resilient so that you achieve an effective stroke even when the shuttle is not struck by the centre of the strings. Nylon gives less tolerance; the poorer quality tends to be quite wooden away from the centre. But nylon usually lasts very much longer than gut, and does not break so easily if you mis-hit the shuttle. If you think you will be keen on playing and can afford gut, I would advise you to buy it. However, if you are uncertain about your interest in the game or would prefer not to pay the extra for gut, buy the best nylon that you can afford. You can always have the racket re-strung with gut during a subsequent season. It is worthwhile having a look at the holes in the frame through which the gut passes. On the inside and outside they should be smooth as any roughness will wear through the stringing very quickly.

The controversy, steel or wood shaft, is now over and steel has won. I need say no more. You can break either shaft quite easily if you play strokes with a whipping action—I mean the action which produces a sharp crack from a whip. The rackets are quite strong enough for normal use, but will not stand the strain of repeated actions such as this.

A new racket has recently been produced in which the shaft and frame are all made of steel. Because the frame is stronger than wood it may be strung more tightly and in these circumstances nylon becomes highly satisfactory. The rackets are very light, less than 4 oz. It seems likely that other rackets of this type will be developed. The lightness should be of advantage to those who are not physically strong but who, nevertheless, have the power to generate a considerable pace if they have a light enough instrument. With such a light racket timing becomes very important and it may require some practice if you have previously played with a heavier racket. Wristy players may gain most advantage because the wrist movement can be held back until very late. It may also mean that players with weaker wrists, who could not play wristy shots with the heavier rackets, may now do so with these light ones.

A badminton racket is strong, but delicate. It needs to be looked after. *Do* put it in a press between club nights, and for obvious reasons don't keep it in a place that is either very dry or very damp.

Dress

Badminton clubs usually insist on their members wearing white, although why this should be so (apart from aesthetic reasons) I have never understood. The clothes should be loose enough to permit freedom of movement, but not so loose that they become a nuisance. I mention this only because I have seen ladies lose a point because there was a bundle of skirt between their racket and the shuttle. Several manufacturers produce clothes that are absolutely ideal. My wife's experience suggests that ladies should write to manufacturers for catalogues before visiting shops. She has found that even the best sports shops are only too willing to say that what they happen to have in stock are the only clothes produced by brand 'x' whereas the catalogue shows a much wider range. A warm cardigan or sweater is essential for wear while you are knocking up and to put on again after an energetic game; badminton halls are not the warmest of places.

The socks should help to cushion the feet and should be of a design that will not slip down under the heel. Experience is the only guide here, because I find that people vary so much in the type of sock they find ideal.

The shoes should have a definite pattern on the sole to provide a secure grip. Badminton demands lots of sudden starts and stops, twists and turns. If your shoes tend to slip you will find it difficult to play the game. Some players wear away the soles quickly, others rub the toe-cap and sides of the shoes, while others have the happy knack of separating the upper from the sole. The more expensive shoes are strengthened at these various points to give a longer life. But because they are so well made they tend to be heavier than others. If you know the parts of the shoe that you wear badly, you will probably have found a make that gives you the best service. If you have no experience I suggest that you start with an inexpensive pair and hope that they meet your needs. It is essential that the shoes should have cushioned insoles, because you will need to bounce about the court. Sore feet and good badminton do not go together.

It may seem pernickety to suggest that you should also buy some shoe-cleaner with your shoes. It always seems odd that players turn up in beautifully white sweaters, shorts, etc., but forget to clean their shoes and so completely spoil the picture.

Etiquette

When I see the word 'etiquette' I always think how old-fashioned and Victorian it seems, yet in club games, matches and tournaments it is so obviously a social asset. And how difficult it is for a club secretary or team captain to put a player on the right path! It is very tempting to produce a list of questions, and award marks for the answers. The totals could give a range of assessments from 'impossibly good' to 'impossibly rude'. But this would make matters unnecessarily complicated, when all that is required is normal good manners. For example, if you are passing a shuttle to a player, he should not have to pick it up off the floor because of your carelessness. Don't serve until you have looked to see that both your opponents are ready. It is not only rude to serve before your opponents are ready, it is also against the laws of the game. If you are having an 'off day' during which nothing seems to go right for you, try to avoid taking it out on the shuttle, your partner, the equipment, etc. You are the only one to blame. If a linesman or an umpire gives a decision against you which you believe to be wrong, getting angry about it will only interfere with your concentration of the game. Displaying your anger by bad behaviour not only indicates your inability to cope with the situation, but also loses you the sympathy of the spectators and of the linesmen and umpire who, after all, are only human, and are doing their best to see that the competition is fair. You may think that the sympathy of the spectators is unimportant. Ask any under-dog who has suddenly realized that the crowd is with him. The crowd's influence has carried more than one player to success.

Be considerate to poorer players. They may not give you much of a game but if you, and they, do not enjoy it the fault is most likely to be yours. Nancy Horner, who played for Scotland and Middlesex and was, in her day, one of the finest players in the country, brought an atmosphere of competition to any game in which she played. Even the poorest players were stimulated to play their best. Not only did they leave the court feeling that they had played a game of badminton with a capital B, but they also knew that Nancy herself had enjoyed it. If you are one of the lesser lights in your club, be sure to balance any game you make up to ensure that there are two pairs of even strength. If you know that an important club match or tournament is coming up avoid picking those who are likely to be involved, because they will want to sharpen their game on each other.

No comments on etiquette would be complete without some references to timekeeping. I knew of a club which played in the first division of a county league. Those playing for it were county, near county or ex-county players. They were invariably twenty minutes late for their home fixtures because they had gone home to have a meal before the match. The visiting team had usually travelled a good distance, having snatched something to eat on the way, and eventually returned home after the match in the early hours of the morning.

Many tournaments run to a tight schedule and no tournament secretary likes having to scratch a player. Time after time, players turn up with no real reason for being late and get very annoyed if they are scratched. That so few are scratched is a compliment to the long-suffering patience of many tournament organizers and referees.

Scoring

Scoring seems odd at first, but it is, once you get used to it, quite easy. One point is particularly important: a side may add to its score only when it is serving.

If for example the game is doubles, one player will continue to serve while his side continues to win. When it loses a rally the other player, his partner, serves until it again loses a rally; the service then passes to the opponents. The opponents continue to serve until each player has lost his service, when the service returns to the first pair. So that the players may be reminded who has, or has not served, the umpire in a match adds 'first server', 'second server' or 'service over', as appropriate, to the score.

At the beginning of each doubles' game, the side which serves first has only one service (see Law 11).

There is one further slight complication connected with serving. At the beginning of the game, play always starts with a service from the right-hand court to the diagonally opposite court. Thereafter the service is from alternate sides. In singles this means that when a player wins a service during a game he will continue serving from where he left off; thus he will serve from the right service court if his score is even, and from the left if it is odd. In case I've put this too briefly, let me explain further. If a player wins the first rally of the game, having served from the right court, his next service at 1–0 will be from the left court. His third service from the right at 2–0. Thus he is always serving from the left court when his score is odd and from the right court when his score is even. This ensures the continuation of the service from the correct side. In doubles the situation is complicated by the presence of a partner, but again there are simple rules to help you to remember who should start serving again when your side wins the service. When the game starts in doubles, whoever is occupying the right-hand court will always occupy that court when his side's score is even. Needless to say, the phrase 'always occupy that court' refers only to serving and receiving service; once play starts both players are free to move anywhere within their court. There are two particular occasions when you will want to know which court to occupy.

(*a*) When you win the service. If your score is *even*, whoever started the game in the right-hand court should serve from that court. If your score is *odd* the player who occupied the left-hand court at the beginning of the game should serve from the *right-hand court*.

(*b*) When you are receiving service. If your score is even, the player who first served from the right-hand court will receive service in that court. If the score is *odd*, his partner will receive service in the *right-hand court*.

In all doubles and men's singles the game is 15 points, with setting at 13-all or 14-all. The side that first reaches 13 or 14 has the choice of setting or not. If the setting is at 13-all, the game is extended to 18, although in practice the score becomes 'love all', and the winners are the first side to reach 5. At 14-all, the game is extended to 17, and again the score becomes 'love-all' and the first pair to reach 3 wins the game. Of course, if a game should reach 13- or 14-all, and the pair with the option decide not to set, the game goes to the usual 15 points.

In ladies' singles the game consists of 9 points with somewhat similar arrangements for setting. When the score reaches 9-all, the player who first reached 9 has the option of setting the game to 3. At 10-all, the player who first reached 10 has the option of setting to 2.

The Grip

When I first began to play badminton, it seemed odd that players should bother about how to grip a racket. After all, nobody had shown me how to grip a ball when I wanted to throw it or how to hold a bat for rounders, which I had played at a fairly tender age. But perhaps I had simply forgotten any instructions I might have been given. However, my experience as both player and coach has shown quite clearly that there are

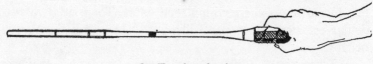

2a Forehand grip

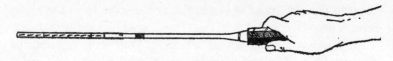

2b Backhand grip

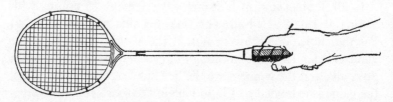

2c Panhandle or frying-pan grip

advantages in holding the racket one way, and disadvantages in holding it another.

Figure 2 (*a*) illustrates the forehand grip which is used for playing all strokes on the right-hand side and also those directly overhead. This grip allows the player to take full advantage of the flexibility of his wrist. When the arm is stretched, the racket should form a continuation of the arm, the wrist should not be cocked up so that the racket slopes up from the arm. During play, of course, the wrist will be twisted in all kinds of directions, but when the racket hits the shuttle the arm, hand and racket should form a straight line. Have a look at figure 5 (*d*).

Most players change their grip to that shown in figure 2 (*b*) for the backhand stroke. The difference is slight but significant. If the racket is held in a forehand grip and is twisted a quarter of a turn to the right, it should be in place for you to take a backhand grip. If you take a normal forehand grip again and this time twist the racket a quarter of a turn with your left hand so that the grip slips round in the fingers of your right hand without turning that hand, you should have the racket and hand in the correct position for backhand strokes. It is easy to check. Stretch your right arm and the racket out in front of you. The back of the hand should be parallel to the ceiling. The thumb should lie along a flat side of the grip of the racket. The head of the racket should be almost vertical. Have a look at figures 7 (*a*) to (*e*).

There is a third grip used in badminton, particularly for net play, known as the frying-pan or panhandle grip, see figure 2 (*c*). When very little backswing and follow-through are required, e.g. at the net, this is an ideal grip.

Why have different grips? Do you hold a knife and fork and spoon all the same way? Probably the answer is no. Why have different grips for them? Because with each you are performing different but necessary actions. As you will see from the relevant chapters, the forehand and backhand are different actions. The grip for each permits the greatest control, with the greatest power; it also allows a wide variety of strokes to be played. The frying-pan grip is not recommended for powerful strokes, firstly, because there is a risk that the handle of the racket may catch against the wrist during the follow-through, and secondly, because many people are encouraged by it to use the wrong arm action, i.e. that of the dart-thrower rather than that of the tennis-server.

I can recall my astonishment when I was advised to use the backhand grip for backhand strokes. It seemed to me that I had little enough time in which to get the shuttle back without complicating matters further by having to change grips. It took me nearly a season to make the change an automatic one. Thereafter I did not need to think about my grip at all, it seemed to change of itself. I am quite sure that one piece of advice helped enormously. The grip on the racket should never become tight while we are preparing to play a stroke. It will tighten by itself just before the moment of impact so that we need not be afraid of the racket slipping out of our hand. If the grip is loose then the racket may be twisted quickly and efficiently in the fingers.

Writing about the fingers brings me to the last point I want to make about the grip. In the forehand grip, the index finger should be further up the handle of the racket than the thumb. In the backhand grip the index finger is lower down the handle than the thumb.

2

STROKES

THIS CHAPTER is included as a prelude to a detailed considera-
tion of badminton, because the game, like any other, has its
own jargon. But it is confined to strokes because I want you to
get a clear mental picture of them so that you can read critically
the remainder of the book. I hope, for example, that while reading about a forehand overhead clear in later chapters your
mind will already be considering the overhead drop shot and
the smash. Thus when you come to tactics you should have an
understanding of the strokes and their purpose and again you
can read critically what I have written. And do read critically.
Challenge, in your mind, the ideas that are presented because it
is this challenge that will ensure the development of your game
and of the game of badminton as a whole. I have tried to be
conscious of any prejudices I have and to avoid them. It is unlikely, however, that I have wholly succeeded. If you are human,
you also will have prejudices. So if you find yourself rejecting
immediately what I have written, pause and think. For my experience is that this rejection is an indication of prejudice at work.

In badminton it is a fault to let the shuttle touch the floor in
your court during play, therefore all shots have to be taken on
the 'volley'. This greatly simplifies matters because the element
of uncertainty associated with a bounce is removed. But because
there is no bounce the player needs to make the shuttle travel
through the air all the way to the place he wants to reach. The
trajectories and lengths of the basic strokes have been developed
to deal with situations that arise regularly in the game. You will,
of course, see players, good and bad, improvising strokes to
meet particular circumstances.

On the facing page there are two dimensional drawings (height and length) of the various strokes described below. The Third dimension, direction, is best considered in relation to tactics.

Forehand

Overhead Clear

There are two types of overhead clear, defensive and attacking, and in both the shuttle is cleared the whole length of the court. The defensive clear is needed in four situations: when you want to play for time (perhaps because you have been drawn out of position); when you know that your opponent cannot play an effective return from such a long shot; when there is no more effective stroke to play; and when you are fencing with your opponent for an opening. This last situation occurs most frequently in singles. The shuttle should drop vertically on to the base-line towards which it is being played. A shuttle falling in this way is often difficult to time and has no speed that the opposing player may use when playing the return.

The object of the attacking clear is to get the shuttle past your opponent, over his head, before he can strike it, and thus force him to play a difficult hurried stroke. It is a particularly useful stroke in singles to stretch and tire an opponent. It is also valuable in doubles, particularly if it is disguised so that the opponents expect some other stroke. It may be a disadvantage if you play it when off-balance or out of position, unless it is an outright winner, because your opponent can use the speed of the shuttle to play a quick return out of your reach.

As you will see from the diagrams the defensive clear reaches quite a height before dropping vertically. The higher it goes, the longer is the time the player has to recover from the difficult situation which prompted the stroke. A shuttle dropping from a height is difficult to time, hence the higher the shot the better. The attacking clear should be just beyond the reach of your opponent.

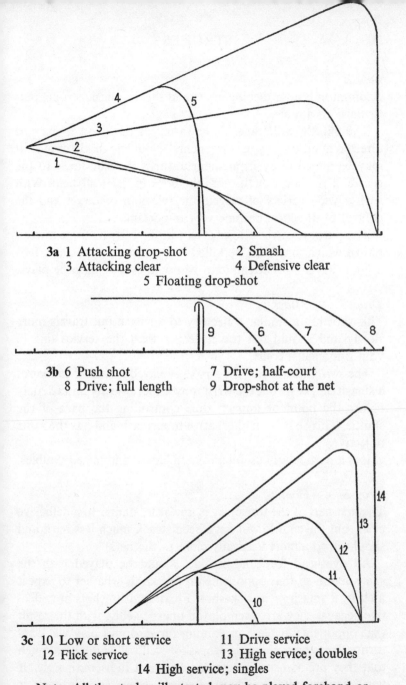

3a 1 Attacking drop-shot   2 Smash
       3 Attacking clear   4 Defensive clear
               5 Floating drop-shot

3b 6 Push shot   7 Drive; half-court
       8 Drive; full length   9 Drop-shot at the net

3c 10 Low or short service   11 Drive service
       12 Flick service   13 High service; doubles
               14 High service; singles

Note: All the strokes illustrated may be played forehand or
backhand

3 Trajectories of strokes

Smash

Badminton is an attacking game and this is a basic stroke, particularly in doubles.

The shuttle will travel downwards all the way; it may be directed at either of your opponents' shoulders, body or legs; it may be aimed away from them towards the side lines, to the centre of the court or towards the floor in front of them. With such a wide variety of targets the selection of target and the control of direction become very important.

The purpose of the stroke is to win the rally or force a weak return which may then be killed by you or your partner. It is a poor player who attempts to win with every smash he plays.

Drop-Shot—Attacking

This shot has a similar trajectory to a smash but travels more slowly and should not travel deeper than the service line in your opponent's court.

The swing with which the stroke is played is similar to that of a smash or a clear but the wrist moves more slowly immediately before the point of impact, thus controlling the pace of the shuttle. This shot is an alternative to a smash and has the same objective.

It is a particularly useful stroke in ladies' and mixed doubles.

Drop-Shot—Floating

The first part of the trajectory is upwards, similar to a defensive clear, but the shuttle will have been struck much less hard and should drop almost vertically close to the net.

All overhead forehand strokes should be played with the same action so that opponents do not know whether to expect a clear, a smash or a drop-shot. Floating drop-shots are effective because they are often played unexpectedly, with the result that opponents are late in coming forward and play weak returns. Those who play this drop-shot well will enjoy it so much that they are sometimes tempted to use it indiscriminately. If you enjoy using it, a good test of your discrimination is to count how many rallies you lose when you play one or more drop-shots.

Backhand

Overhead

There is a similar range of overhead strokes on the backhand; these are often referred to as high backhand strokes. Most players have much less powerful backhands than forehands so that smashes are less often played backhand. Instead the shuttle is played with a forehand stroke high but to the left of the player. These are known as round-the-head strokes.

Drives

A drive may be played with equal facility on the forehand and backhand. Basically it is a stroke in which the shuttle is driven horizontally at about shoulder-level, but it may be played downwards from slightly above shoulder-level or upwards from about waist-level. The direction and length will depend on the circumstances. But if you bear in mind that you may either want to drive the shuttle past your opponent to the back of the court, to drive it at him or make it land about four feet in front of him, you will get some indication of the possibilities. There is always a temptation to hit a drive too hard. If the shuttle is above net-level when it is struck, this may not be a disadvantage, but it often is when the stroke is played from below net-level. As you can imagine, the shuttle is then rising as it passes the net, inviting the opponent to play an attacking downward stroke.

Net Shots

These include a range of strokes, played at the net, in which the shuttle may be played hard onto the floor (if it is above net-level when it is struck) or caressed gently over the net if it has to be played from below net-level. Any net shots played from below net-level must fall as close to the other side of the net as possible, giving the opponent a difficult stroke to play. If the opponent is near the net, the shuttle must be close to the top of the net as it crosses it, otherwise he will step forward and play it sharply onto the floor.

Underarm

High

These are usually returns to smashes or drop-shots. The shuttle may be lifted defensively to fall, like the defensive clear, vertically onto the baseline. It may be driven faster and lower to fulfil the same function as an attacking clear. The purposes are similar to these two strokes.

Low

These strokes can vary from a low drive which skims over the net and may almost reach the back of the court to a drop-shot. The purpose is usually to regain the attack by forcing the opponents to play a high return.

Service

Low

The trajectory is flat. The ideal is to flight the shuttle so that it is above net-level on your side and travels downwards as it crosses the net. This often forces an opponent to play an upward shot in return. The object is to start the rally without giving your opponent any advantage, while retaining for your own side as much advantage as possible.

Drive and Flick

Players of any reasonable standard will move forward and try to return the low service downwards; they will have to move quickly to achieve this. To temper their enthusiasm, you should be able to play a shot over their heads from a swing similar to that used for the low service. If they do not know which service to expect they will have to refrain from rushing the low service in case you flick the shuttle over their heads.

The trajectory will vary depending upon whether you want to drive the shuttle at about head-level or lift it above the reach of your opponent's racket.

High

This is the basic service in singles. In other games it is an alternative to the low or flick service and is particularly useful when the opponents do not have strong overhead strokes.

The shuttle has a similar trajectory to the high underarm stroke; the length will vary between the baseline (singles) and the back doubles service line (doubles, of course). The shuttle should fall as close to the vertical as possible because it is then difficult to time.

Returns of Service

Net shots or drives may be used against low services; smashes, drop-shots or clears against flick or high services.

Push Shots

These seldom receive the dignity of a separate name but they are such a vital part of play, particularly in mixed doubles, that I feel sure that they should be mentioned separately.

The stroke is played parallel and close to the sideline from approximately one front service line to the other. The shuttle usually flies low over the net past the opposing player. Sometimes it is better to play it higher, just beyond racket reach but in such a way that your opponent is tempted to try to play an impossible shot. The temptation is usually the slow speed of the shuttle.

If you acquire the full range of strokes that have been described here you will be well on the way to being a *good* player. If you lack some of the strokes or do not play some of them well, you will have difficulty in being a *very good* player.

3

FOOTWORK

AMONG COACHES THERE is often a 'which came first' argument as to which should be taught first, the footwork of a stroke or the stroke itself. Each coach decides the answer on the basis of his experience and the aptitude of the pupils he is teaching. In my experience it is very difficult to improve the footwork of a player who has been playing long enough to develop habits. I do not know the reason for this, but my guess is that people do not need to give much thought to their feet in getting from one part of the court to another. After all they have walked and run about since they were young children and you are merely asking them to use a skill they already possess, one which they are confident they can use. It is also difficult to demonstrate that a player's footwork is poor because so many people seem to be unable to 'observe' what their feet are doing when they are moving about the court. It is easy to demonstrate the difficulties players may get into because of bad footwork. This, however, usually leads to a request to be taught to play impossible shots from impossible situations.

The earlier you acquire good patterns of footwork, the easier it will be for you to be in the right place at the right time, with your feet in the right position for a particular stroke.

There are some principles worth noting:

1. When a rally is about to start or is in progress you should never let your weight sink back onto your heels. The weight should always be forward on the balls of your feet.

2. When stationary during a rally, try to keep your knees slightly bent. Before you can move you will almost certainly have to bend them and the fraction of a second you lose may

well make the difference between a kill and a defensive shot.

3. You should always try to move faster than the shuttle so that you can balance yourself to play the shuttle and immediately move, or be ready to move for the next shot. This is particularly important when moving backwards to play the shuttle overhead.

4. During most strokes, particularly powerful ones, the weight is transferred from one foot to the other. Make sure that the foot that is to receive your weight is on, or very close to, the ground before impact.

Readiness to Move

If you want to move backwards or forwards as quickly as possible, the best ready position is with the feet fore and aft. Similarly if the movement is to be sideways, the feet should be in line with the direction of the movement. In a game of badminton, when you know the direction in which you will have to move you should adjust your feet to the 'best' position. For instance, your feet should be fore and aft when you are receiving service; they should be side by side at the net if the shuttle may come to either side of you. There will be times, e.g. when your opponent is in a position to play a smash, a clear or a drop-shot, when you will not know the direction in which you will need to move until the opponent has struck the shuttle. In this case players usually compromise. If they are defending on the backhand, the right foot is usually moved up to a foot forward; the feet remain about a shoulder's width apart (see figure 4). If you want to receive the smash on the forehand the left foot is moved forward in the same way.

4 Defensive stance against attack which will probably come on the backhand side

There is a risk for men in mixed doubles in moving the right foot forward. The shoulders turn with the feet and a shuttle flying high to the backhand is often played backhand because the eyes, following the shuttle, turn the shoulders farther round to the left. Once this stage is reached, few players may recover to play a forehand, but few players have such a good backhand that they can afford to use it instead of the much stronger forehand. If you have this habit, or find yourself developing it, try to make sure that your shoulders turn to the right immediately you begin to move back to play the shuttle. You will then move into a position to play a forehand stroke.

Movement

There are almost as many ways of moving about the court as there are badminton players. Nevertheless they can be broken down into types. At the one extreme is the tall player who covers the court with a single step and a reach and who never seems to move quickly. The best of them are always in plenty of time to play the shot; the worst are no worse than any others. At the other extreme is the 'bluebottle' who seems to spend his game buzzing about the court with enormous industry. Again the best are very effective, while the worst always need a yard or so to recover, having struck the shuttle as they passed by it. In between the two extremes is the ideal who takes long or short, fast or slow strides according to the demands of the particular stroke. Usually they accelerate by using small steps and take a long stride to play the stroke. Watch a good singles player moving into the net to play an underarm defensive stroke against a drop-shot. He gets no closer to the net than he needs because he knows only too well that he will have to come back to his base in the centre of the court. Three words I would commend to you—economy of effort.

You must also move immediately you receive the 'signal' to do so. Have you ever watched the start of a 100-yards sprint or a swimming race? All are ready to start; their 'springs' are coiled to project them forward as soon as the starter's pistol is fired. In badminton the signal isn't usually so obvious, but immediately you get it you must move. This applies to any of you, whether or not you are by nature or by training a fast mover. There is a lesson to be learned from a 100-yards sprint test carried out by a well-known football club. Those who were recognized as being among the fastest movers on the football field proved to be comparatively slow runners. But their anticipation and speed of reaction more than made up for any deficiency in their running speed.

Another method of increasing the apparent speed about the court is to move immediately you play a stroke. The movement must be towards the base that will give you the best opportunity for dealing with probable returns. If you have not reached the base before your opponent strikes the shuttle you must pause, momentarily, while he plays his stroke, otherwise you may find yourself moving in the wrong direction. While your clear is travelling the length of the court there is ample time to move two or three steps from the back of the court to the centre. You will see in the illustrations of the forehand clear that the feet move forward two steps. Thus, if this stroke is played correctly, the player should be well on his way to some place near the centre of the court. Similarly a full backhand stroke should turn the shoulders until they are facing the net, which will pull the right foot towards the centre of the court. At this stage, when the shuttle has been sent on its way and the stroke is completed, many people pause to admire their handiwork. I have become convinced that they are quite unaware of doing this, that it started when they were unsure of their shots and has now become a habit. It is a habit that may be broken only by a determined mental effort. Start with one stroke (e.g. moving into the net after a low service, or moving forward after a clear). Ask a friend to watch whether you do in fact move after hitting the shuttle.

The immediate benefit of moving to your base after playing a stroke is that you will have more time in which to prepare for the next stroke. But it is difficult for many people to judge whether they have moved to the best base in preparation for the return; and it is very difficult to provide any specific advice because there are so many variables in the game which give rise to a wide variety of situations. However, you can readily make some assessment of particular situations by making a rough plan of the court, drawing lines to represent possible returns and then selecting places on the court to which you (and your partner) could move. If you do this shortly after playing a game in which you felt you had not been covering the court well, it can directly benefit your game.

Have you ever watched players moving back to play a shuttle overhead? My observations show that in many cases the players move quickly if the shuttle is moving quickly and slowly if the shuttle is slow. In both cases they do not move back far enough to play forward into the shuttle. Thus the delightful theory that I was propounding a few paragraphs back has gone for a burton because the player is not going to be able to take two steps forward as he plays the stroke and thus 'be well on his way' to his base. More likely he will be struggling to get *back* into the court before sprinting for the next stroke, and because he will be late for that stroke he is almost certain to be racing for the next, and so on. The Khans are a family of champion squash players. While giving a demonstration one of them commented that a player needed to move faster than the ball if he was going to be in the right place at the right time. The same rule applies to badminton. But it takes a long time to alter habits of movement. If you decide to alter yours, start with the least difficult situation—a high service or a high clear. Make sure that you move back beyond the shuttle and be conscious of moving forward into the shuttle as you play your stroke.

Now let's think about specific foot movements on the court. Imagine you are playing a singles and that you are standing with feet apart in the centre of the court. Your opponent plays a good drop-shot from the back of the court to the left-hand corner of the net. Moving in to play the backhand underarm return you would probably take a short step with your right, a slightly longer one with your left and finally a long one with your right, reaching forward to play the stroke as you do so.

The right leg will finish bent and be the spring to push you back towards the centre of the court. The movement towards the net on the forehand side is similarly right, left, right. This may seem odd, but with the right foot forward the player has the longest possible reach with his right hand, therefore his feet travel a shorter distance using this sequence.

Movement across the court to play a drive is left, right to the backhand and right, left towards the forehand. Often, however, in moving towards the forehand a player will move his left foot up to his right and then take a step with his right to play the stroke because this saves time but still provides plenty of power. Do remember when moving across, also to move diagonally forward to meet the shuttle early.

When going back to play an overhead forehand stroke you may either chassé or run backwards. (Chassé is a gliding step— well known to ballroom dancers—in which, if one foot takes a step, the other foot is drawn up to it, but never passes it. Several chassé steps may be taken in sequence.) The object is to get behind the shuttle so that you can play a controlled stroke forward into the shuttle. The chassé method is better because it turns the shoulders to the right to the best position for playing the stroke. The movement backwards should end with the weight on the right foot ready for the forward swing described in Chapter 4.

It may be argued that in a game you will seldom start moving from the ideal position of a definite base. This may well be so. But it in no way invalidates the proposition that you should aim to achieve economy of effort by well-organized foot movements. For example, if you play a straight smash from the backhand corner in mixed doubles and have to move forward to a low straight return that gets past your partner, you will almost certainly move right, left, right as the singles player did in going in to the net. If you have to move across the full width of the court you will have to add additional steps to the ones I have mentioned for the drive but they should be those you would use to recover from your previous stroke. Of course you may be pulled out of position, of course you may be caught by a deceptive shot and in both cases be only too thankful to scramble back somehow. But these should be exceptions.

If you want to have good footwork, you need to practise—unless you are one of the gifted few. The chances of practice during a game are not many. But you can do a lot when you are knocking up beforehand, or when you go to pick up the shuttle in between points. You can do a bit at home or on an empty court. Try moving to play forehand and backhand drives alternately, chasséing back to play a clear and moving forward to your base again, going forward to the net and backing out again. Repeat the moves until the footwork becomes habitual. Then you will see the improvement in your game!

4

FOREHAND STROKES

THESE ARE FUNDAMENTAL strokes because they will make up sixty to seventy per cent of your game. If you master them you will be well on your way to becoming a good badminton player. Different people progress at different speeds. Men, for example, find them fairly easy, because the basis is a throwing action and as boys they spent a lot of time throwing things. But ladies seem to have less cause to throw things and often find that either the basic action takes some time to master or not enough power is available without lots of practice. However, if you go about these strokes in the right way you will find that both difficulties are considerably reduced.

The basic overhead forehand swing is illustrated in figures 5 (a) to 5 (e). Try your own swing and watch your arm as you do so. If your swing closely resembles that in the illustrations, well and good. If you are in doubt, go quickly through the instructions on the swing given below, checking up as you do so. Where you find radical differences, it is highly probable that you need to change. The illustrations represent the important stages in the swing; if there are differences at any of these stages it is advisable to change.

Do remember in all the strokes in this chapter that the arm should be at full stretch at the moment of impact, and that you should be playing forward into the shuttle. You should be holding the racket in a forehand grip.

The following paragraphs have been written in a 'teach-yourself' pattern for the many who will want coaching either because they are learning the game or because they want to improve their efficiency. The stroke being taught is the over-

5a   5b

5a to 5e Foreha

head clear in which the shuttle is played the full length of the court. It demands a full swing and strong body movement. Once the former is acquired it can easily be adapted for forehand strokes at other levels all of which utilize the same swing. Most of the steps in the instruction can be practised off the court.

The Swing

1. Stand on your toes with your feet together, straighten your arms and wrist and reach as high as you can above your head. Make sure that there is a straight line from your feet to the tip of your racket [see figure 5 (*d*)]. This is how you should be at the moment you strike the shuttle for the overhead clear. For the smash you will be leaning forward a little.

5c   5d   5e

erhead clear

2. Now bend your elbow and let the head of the racket touch your back between the shoulder blades, lowering your heels to the ground as you do so.

3. Throw the racket head up to the position in Step 1. You need not stop the racket when you are at full stretch but let it follow through, making sure that it goes down your left side. Try this a few times. Make it a loose, relaxed action and gradually increase the pace of the swing.

4. Now take a step forward with your left foot; keep the toes pointing forwards but turn the top half of your body to the right.

5. Put the racket in the position of Step 2. Check with figure 5 (*a*). Now throw the racket head up to reach the point of impact in Step 1. The action will pull the right shoulder round and the right foot forward. It is essential that the arm should

be straightening while the shoulders are turning. Try this a few times, slowly at first but gradually quickening the swing.

6. Standing as in Step 4, raise your arm sideways until it reaches shoulder level. At this point the upper arm remains still while the elbow bends to drop the racket head behind your back. You are now in the position at the beginning of Step 5. Try repeating this until it feels a natural movement but instead of just raising your arm swing it back and up. Make the whole movement smooth and controlled.

7. Now add Step 5 to this swing. Remember to follow through down your left side. As you follow through your right foot will come forward as in figure 5 (e).

Now let's try hitting the shuttle, but don't be *too* intent upon hitting it or you will probably not swing the racket at all well and at this stage it is important that you develop a good stroke. If you can hang a shuttle at the height of your point of impact and practise hitting it you will avoid rush. If, however, this is impossible, get a friend to stand about eight feet in front of you and throw the shuttle up into the air so that it will drop almost on top of your head. A little practice is needed to do this well. It is important that the shuttle is thrown twelve to fifteen feet in the air to give you time to make a full swing. Now step back with your right foot, ask your friend to throw the shuttle and swing your racket to hit it—not too hard. It does not matter at this stage where it goes provided that you are hitting it with the relaxed full swing you were practising. As your confidence and ability increase, try to hit the shuttle harder by doing Step 5 more and more quickly.

This then is the basic swing for the forehand overhead clear. Try practising it on a court as soon as possible. Add in the chasséing movement mentioned in Chapter 3, and make sure that you move back faster than the shuttle whenever possible.

Direction

This is controlled by the face of the racket and by the point of impact. The face must be at right-angles to the direction in which you want the shuttle to go and may be controlled by the wrist, the arm or the shoulders. Let me explain. Hold your racket in a forehand grip, turn your wrist to the right until the palm of your hand is facing upwards; the face of the racket should now be parallel to the ceiling. Keep the forearm stationary and play an imaginary soft shot up into the air using your wrist to move the racket. Still keeping the forearm stationary play an imaginary stroke, using your wrist, to your right and then to your left. This will give you some indication of the extent to which you can rely on your wrist for direction. If you have a free movement in both directions you are lucky. The majority will find that they have to turn their forearm as well as the wrist. You will probably also find that the freedom of the movement is greater if you are relaxed and your grip is loose. If you are playing the strokes correctly the wrist provides a flick immediately before impact with the shuttle. Thus if you can change a direction with the wrist (and forearm), your opponents will have the shortest possible notice of your intentions. But if you turn your shoulders to alter direction, you are forecasting well in advance. There may be occasions when you will do this. Perhaps you have found a weakness in your opponent's defence and decide that you will cause him the maximum of discomfort by hammering that weakness. You may well add to that discomfort by making the direction of your shot obvious. Against better players this will probably not work because the notice will enable them to improvise another return.

Other Overhead Strokes

The downward stroke is called a smash, a most descriptive name. It is *the* point-winning stroke in most badminton. You must learn to direct the shuttle to the right and left or directly at your opponent; to alter the height so that it will be at floor, knee, waist, chest or head level when it reaches him.

Use the same action as you did for the clear. But your point of impact should be in front of you, as in a tennis service, and not above your right shoulder as in the clear.

The last overhead stroke is a drop-shot which may be 'fast' (in fact a slow version of the smash, landing near the front service line) or 'floating'. The floating drop-shot, particularly valuable in singles, travels upwards in the first part of its flight but, because it is played gently, drops almost vertically close to the net—on your opponent's side, of course. The most common method of playing the drop-shot is to check the forward movement of your wrist just before impact, almost as if you wanted to frighten the shuttle, but not hit it. The swing up to the check is exactly the same as was used for other overhead strokes; thus your opponent should not know until the last moment which stroke to expect.

An alternative method of playing the stroke is to brush the racket sharply across the base of the shuttle. The movement is controlled by the wrist and takes place at the top of the swing. It requires a lot of practice but is most effective. Right-handed players find it easiest to move the racket from right to left.

Right-handed players may also develop a drop-shot which will be played from the back right-hand side of the court to the left-hand corner of the net. The swing is exactly the same as that used for a clear; there should be no check or slowing down of the movement. The point of contact is almost directly above, or slightly in front of the right shoulder. The opponent is led by the swing to expect a hard straight shot but at the last moment the racket face slices from left to right across the face of the shuttle instead of striking the shuttle squarely. The shuttle will fly quite quickly across the court to the left-hand corner of the net. Provided that you play the shot confidently, it is easy, but practice is necessary if the stroke is to become accurate and reliable.

A cross-court drop-shot may be played in the reverse direction from the backhand side by slicing from right to left, but most players find this shot more difficult because the swing is not quite such a natural one. From the left-hand corner most cross-court drop-shots will be played by turning the wrist at the moment of impact.

The overhead shots considered so far have all referred to

situations in which the shuttle is struck while directly above, or in front of, the right shoulder or else a little farther to the right. If the shuttle has to be taken high but well to the right, there is a risk that it will be hit hard and consistently into the net because the natural follow-through for this stroke is sharply downwards. To eliminate the fault, the follow-through must be flattened. But it need not be as flat when you are close to the net as when you are near the back of the court.

a   **b**

6a & 6b Forehand round-the-head stroke

Overhead shots on the opposite side of the body, i.e. above the head or to the left almost down to shoulder-level, may also be played forehand. The action is the same as for other overhead shots, but the body should be bent towards the left and the head also bent a little to the left to allow the arm to remain as straight as possible [see figures 6 (*a*) and 6 (*b*)]. If you have difficulty in making the swing correctly, try the following sequence to get the feel of it.

1. Stretch your arm vertically above your right shoulder.

2. Bend it at the elbow so that the forearm rests on your head.

3. Move the forearm backwards and downwards until your hand touches the back of your neck [see figure 6 (*a*)].

4. Now throw your hand up, as if to hit a shuttle to the left and a little above your head. Try doing this at various levels.

5. Now add this swing (slowly at first) onto the back swing described earlier in this chapter.

To play the shot on the court you need to move the left foot farther to the left than for the other overhead strokes.

There is a risk in using round-the-head strokes that you may try to hit the shuttle too hard and the effort will pull you far across to the left, off-balance. Let me illustrate. Two very good international ladies' pairs met in a tournament. For much of the game there was little between them. Then one of the ladies, with a particularly good smash began to hit her round-the-head shots so hard that she had difficulty in recovering to reach a cross-court return. For the next half-dozen points she found herself deep in the left-hand corner playing round-the-head smashes. The opponent returned the shuttle farther and farther to the left until the attacker became slightly off-balance. The shuttle was then driven across court past and to the left of her partner at the net. Those six points were vital because, although she changed her tactics, she could not make up the leeway.

Provided round-the-head strokes are used with discretion they have all the advantages of power and variety of the other overhead strokes. Do learn to play them; do learn to use them properly.

Strokes at Shoulder-level

Having learned an overhead stroke, you can now use the same swing for a drive. Imagine that you want to strike a shuttle at arm's length to your right, a little in front of you and at shoulder-level. You will have to step across towards the shuttle with your left foot, cocking your arm as you did for the clear then throwing the racket horizontally at the shuttle. By 'cocking', I mean swinging the racket backwards then bending the elbow so that the racket head drops behind the back.

If you prefer slightly more detailed instruction, and most people understandably do, follow the steps below.

Remember—during most of this stroke the arm will be at shoulder-level.

1. Stand with your feet apart as if you were facing the right side line. Raise your right arm, hand and racket sideways to shoulder-level. The arm and the racket should now form a straight line with your shoulders.

2. Bend the right elbow and let the racket touch your back between the shoulder-blades.

3. Swing the arm as if to hit the shuttle at shoulder-level opposite your left shoulder. You will find that as you do so your shoulders will turn to the left. This is the same swing as you used for the overhead strokes, but at a lower level.

4. Start again with your feet apart, but this time take a pace forward with your left foot. As you do so, put the racket behind your shoulders as in Step 2, and then swing as in Step 3. You will find that the right foot is dragged towards the left. Repeat this several times until it feels under control and then if possible practise hitting a shuttle in the way that I suggested for the overhead stroke. The person who is throwing the shuttle should stand directly in front of you, about eight feet away, and throw it fairly slowly in an arc out to your right. You must not hurry the stroke until you are confident of your ability to play it, and therefore it is important that the shuttle be thrown slowly to begin with.

In a game you would normally be facing the net and would have to turn and move to the right before playing the stroke. Try this now. Be sure that, as you begin to turn, the back-swing also begins so that you are fully prepared to play the shuttle when the time comes.

Now practise using this swing to hit shuttles at different levels above and below shoulder height. Having acquired a good swing there is a slight modification—indeed, a simplification—that you should incorporate in all strokes that are not overhead ones. Watch the good players: it is seldom that the racket goes as far back as the shoulders. In fact the length of the back-swing depends on their strength and the time they have available. What they do is to swing the racket far enough back to enable them to hit the shuttle to any part of their opponent's court. Thus they try to prevent the opponent from anticipating correctly the shot they intend to play. This should be your objective also.

A similar modification may be made to overhead strokes which are played about mid-court. In this case the back-swing is not down, back and up; there usually is not time. Instead the racket is lifted sideways, dropped behind the head and then thrown at the shuttle. Be sure that the upper arm swings backward, turning the shoulders to the right, as you place the racket behind your head. You can check this for yourself; does your elbow point towards the net when the racket is behind your head? If it does, your right arm has not swung backwards. The elbow should point to the side line or towards the back of the court at this stage of the swing.

Underarm Strokes

If you play golf, you will find these underarm strokes very similar in form to the golf swing, with two exceptions—you will only use one hand of course, and a full swing is never used.

Put the racket behind the shoulders as you would for a full-blooded drive. Have your shoulders facing towards the side line and your feet fore and aft as for the clear. Lower the elbow until it is pointing towards the ground, but keep it and the wrist bent. The head of the racket should now be near the right shoulder. The shuttle has to be struck at about knee-level, and in front and a little to the right of the player. So swing the arm down and forward turning the chest towards the net as you do so. During this forward swing the arm should straighten and the racket be thrown underarm at the shuttle. The follow-through is upwards and a little towards the left. If it were allowed to

continue, the right hand would reach the left ear. A similar
swing to this is used for the high service.

In the backswing, the racket should be swung back and under;
the elbow is fully bent by the time the upper part of the arm is
pointing downwards at an angle of forty-five degrees to the
vertical. During the forward movement the wrist is held back
until the last moment, when it flicks the racket through.

When there is no time for a full swing the upper arm remains
vertical with the elbow pointing downwards, while the elbow
and wrist first lift the racket sideways and upwards and then
swing it downwards and forwards to strike the shuttle. The
racket is accelerated very rapidly on the downswing. In emer-
gencies the movement will be performed with the wrist only.

General

If a player is standing in the ready position and is expecting
the shuttle to come to his forehand, he should have his arm
across his chest with his elbow and wrist bent (see figure 4).
He need only turn his shoulders and place his arm in the appropriate position ready to play an overhead or underarm stroke
or a drive. If he expects to have to play the shuttle above net-
level (e.g. because it is below net-level at the other side of the
net) he can raise his arm even while the opponent is playing his
stroke. Similarly he should lower it if he expects to play a stroke
at knee-level or lower (e.g. because his opponent is in a position to play an attacking stroke).

It is absolutely vital that players make the preparatory movements for the stroke (i.e. the backswing) as they move towards
the shuttle. This has been mentioned before and is so important
that it deserves mention in every chapter however major or
minor its relevance.

Here we must leave the forehand. All forehand strokes are
basically easy once the swing has been mastered. The most common problem is footwork (discussed in Chapter 3), so make sure
that you give as much attention to that as you do to the swing.

5

BACKHAND STROKES

I WILL USE the same pattern for leading you through the backhand as I did for the forehand: a description of the basic swing
which may be adapted for a shot to be hit at any level, and then
a short discussion of the various strokes. But first I had better
remove any backhand worries you may have. The forehand is
easy to play because we have been practising it since we first
threw things out of a pram: we don't really use the backhand
action until we take up racket games. Therefore when we want
to play them we have to learn the backhand swing and practise

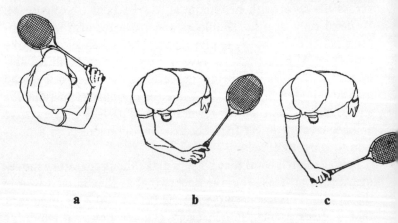

a   b   c

7a to

it until it becomes as natural as the forehand. Once the swing is natural, the stroke is easy.

If you are beginning badminton or are not satisfied with your backhand, it is essential that you go through the following instructions step by step and resist hitting a shuttle until your swing feels relaxed and natural. It will not take a long time. Do watch your arm and wrist as you swing to check that they are in the correct position at each stage.

1. Stand with your feet comfortably apart (about a shoulder's width): imagine that you are facing the left side line, with your right shoulder pointing towards the net. Place the neck of the racket against your left shoulder, raising the right elbow until the right forearm is parallel to the ground [see figure 7 (*a*)].

2. Swing the arm horizontally through a half-circle until it is pointing to the net, straightening the arm gradually during the swing. Watch it as it swings. Repeat several times.

3. This is the basis of the backhand—it's easy, isn't it? Incidentally, you will find that as the arm swings it tends to pull your shoulders round until the chest faces the net. This should happen if the stroke is played correctly.

4. Now cock your wrist as shown in figure 7 (*a*) and place

d   **e**

ackhand drive

the neck of your racket against your left shoulder (as in Step
1 above) and swing your arm again. You will find that your
wrist straightens automatically as you reach the end of the swing.

5. If you were using this swing to hit a shuttle at shoulder-
level, the point of impact would be at arm's length opposite the
right shoulder. This means that the arm and wrist must straighten
as they reach this point. Remember to keep the arm and hand
horizontal. The full swing is shown in figures 7 (*a*) to (*e*). Practise this twenty times.

You may find that the wrist action is rather weak; practice
and exercise will put this right. But before you get on to this
you had better try hitting the shuttle. If you have not played
much badminton try hanging a shuttle at shoulder-level on
about three feet of string. Measure your distance from it by
holding out your arm with your racket in your hand then hit the
shuttle using the swing you have been practising.

You will remember that in the chapter on footwork you
learned to step into the shuttle to play backhand drives. Go
through the movements again just to refresh your memory, for
the next steps combine the arm and foot movements.

(*a*) Stand in the ready position with your racket across your
chest as in figure 4. Make sure that your elbow is bent, your
wrist cocked for a backhand and that you have a backhand
grip.

(*b*) Step across towards the left with your right foot, turning
your shoulders to the left until your right shoulder points to an
imaginary net. As you turn, move your racket up on your
left shoulder and raise your right elbow until the forearm is
horizontal.

(*c*) Swing as if to hit the shuttle. Return to position (*a*) and
repeat until the action flows smoothly. Practise with a moving
shuttle by making your hanging shuttle swing like a pendulum,
parallel to an imaginary side line, and hitting it as it comes
towards you. Next get a friend to throw the shuttle underarm
slowly and diagonally towards your backhand. He should stand
about eight feet away, approximately where the middle of the
net would be. Make sure it travels slowly enough and far

enough to give you time to prepare for the shot. Stand facing
the 'side line' to begin with; then gradually adjust your feet
until you are waiting in the ready position facing the net as you
would be in a game and thus have to make the complete foot,
body and arm motion to hit the shuttle. As you become more
expert, the shuttle should be thrown more and more quickly.
But do make haste slowly. If you try to swing the racket too
quickly before you have reasonable control you are likely to
acquire bad habits, and once you have they are difficult to
eliminate.

At the moment of impact, by the way, the racket, wrist and
arm should, ideally, form a straight line, but there is no great
harm done if there are slight bends at both joints. You will get
little power if the arm is very bent and you are likely to lose
your balance if you really have to stretch to reach the shuttle,
so avoid these extremes.

Wrist Action

Let's make sure you have the correct wrist action. Bend your
elbow a little and cock your wrist as in figure 7 (a). Straighten
the arm fairly quickly, try to keep the wrist cocked until the
arm is almost straight, then make the wrist flick the hand past
the arm. Notice, in figures 7 (c) and (d) that the back of the
hand is horizontal. To begin with you will probably feel
that there is no power in your wrist, but if you can spare a few
minutes each day to practise this action, you will find that
strength and power will develop rapidly.

Strokes at Various Levels

If you want to hit the shuttle at shoulder-level it is important
that you swing the arm at shoulder-level during the whole of
the stroke. Think of your arm as being the spoke of a wheel
that has its centre or hub in your right shoulder.

If the shuttle has to be hit at a higher level than the shoulder
you must tilt the wheel upwards, i.e. point your elbow up.

The hand and racket will then be swung upwards during the first part of the swing and downwards after the shuttle has been struck. For a low shot the elbow should be pointed downwards towards the point at which the shuttle is to be hit. The racket and hand will travel downwards during the first part of the stroke and upwards during the second. If you try this several times you will find that the joints of the elbow and shoulder ensure that your swing is correct, provided you keep the shoulder at the same level during the whole of the swing. Once you have mastered this, all you need concentrate on in the backhand is pointing your elbow towards the correct level (i.e. the level at which the shuttle is going to be struck). Figures 8 (*a*) and (*b*) show the action for the overhead clear.

If the shuttle is to be struck at a point between you and the

a   b

8a & 8b High backhand clear

net you should always move towards it. The actual foot movements will vary with the position from which you start, but do
remember that your object is to take the shuttle as high and as
early as possible. If, however, the shuttle is cleared over your
head and a high backhand stroke has to be played near the back
of your court, you must try to get back quickly enough to be
able to swing forward into the shuttle as described in Chapter
4. The nearer you get to the back of the court the farther your
shoulders must turn to the left and the more of your back you
should show to your opponents. This enables you to use the
twisting action of the body and shoulders to the maximum. It
is worthwhile learning and practising the strokes at various
levels in the same way as you practised the basic swing (i.e.
start at Step 5).

Deception

Do always bear deception in mind. If you take a long swing for
your powerful strokes and a short one for your soft strokes you
might as well shout to your opponent what you are going to
do. Unless you are playing a stroke close to the net always
take a full swing and adjust the power of your stroke by controlling the length and strength of your wrist movement and
also of your follow-through. Try varying these to see what
results you get. Don't expect complete control the first time you
try, but do persist; you will find that it will pay dividends.

Length and Trajectory

So far we have not considered the point to which we are trying to
hit the shuttle. In fact, the points we are aiming at and the
trajectory of the shuttle will be similar to the various shots on
the forehand. For convenience these are repeated in figures 9 (a)
and (b). The occasions when these shots should be played will be
considered under tactics, but it will be useful, at present, to
bear in mind that Shots 1, 5, 6 and 9 will land in front of
your opponent and force him to move towards the net; Shots 7

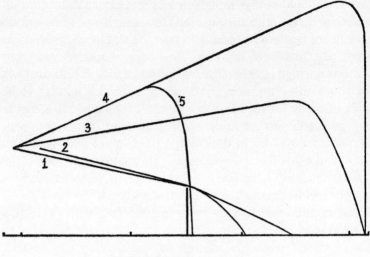

9a 1 Attacking drop-shot
     2 Smash
     3 Attacking clear
     4 Defensive clear
     5 Floating drop-shot

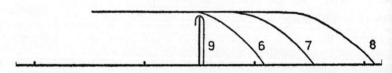

9b 6 Push shot
     7 Drive; half-court
     8 Drive; full length
     9 Drop-shot at the net

9a & **9b** Trajectories of backhand strokes

and 8 will travel down the side line, drawing him towards that side line; Shots 3 and 4 will drive him to the back of the court.

Most people find Shot 4, the backhand overhead clear, rather difficult. It always will be until your wrist is strong enough for you to play the stroke with a wrist and arm movement, but with little assistance from your body. If you strengthen your wrist and use the swing you have been practising, you will find that your difficulties quickly decrease. It is unlikely that you will ever develop a backhand which is as strong as your forehand. So when you are playing to win you should tend to use your forehand instead of your backhand when you have an opportunity to attack the shuttle overhead on the left of the court. You will have to be careful of your footwork, in fact it is so important in this situation that it deserves special comment.

Backhand Clear/Round-the-head Forehand

If you are in the centre of the court and the shuttle is lifted high towards the left, the tendency is to turn the shoulders to the left as your eyes follow the shuttle. Having turned your shoulders to the left you are committed to playing a backhand. If instead of turning your shoulders, you only turned your head and then moved diagonally backwards towards the left you would be in a position to play an effective forehand stroke. Many players will, in fact, avoid playing any high backhands by moving across to play a forehand and they do it most effectively. But, particularly in singles, it is very desirable that you have an effective backhand because you will not usually smash from the back of the court, but will play a clear of a drop-shot. Therefore you have no need to play a forehand provided that you have a good backhand clear or drop-shot.

The backhand drop-shot is played in much the same way as the forehand, i.e. the wrist begins to accelerate as it would for a clear but is slowed down sharply (checked) just before impact. It is unusual to brush across or slice the shuttle on the backhand. But it is much easier to control the wrist—and hence play a deceptive shot—than it is on the forehand.

Defence
When defending against a smash most people find it best to try to take the shuttle on the backhand because a shorter swing is needed, and with practice, a greater area can be protected than with a forehand stroke. You must of course, wait with your

elbow bent ready to play the stroke because you will have little enough time and you don't want to waste any on a backswing. But there is a qualification to all this—you must have a reasonably good back hand otherwise your returns will be too weak to be effective.

Preparation

Preparation for the backhand is all-important unless you do have a very strong wrist. Fortunately preparation is very easy— try it and see. Take a backhand grip on the racket, stand in a position of readiness with the feet apart and the racket across the body and a little way from it (see figure 4). The elbow should be bent to at least ninety degrees. Turn to the left as if to play a backhand shot, keeping your arm in the ready position. Raise your arm, wrist and racket to shoulder level. You should now be in a position to play a backhand drive (subject to a slight adjustment to suit your individual method). Provided that you take the racket with you when you turn to play a backhand you should always be ready to play the stroke; but if you leave it behind, you will always find yourself 'snatching' at the shuttle and playing poor shots.

Errors

There are a few basic errors that creep into many player's backhands while they are developing the stroke. All of them are easy to diagnose and if you are willing to concentrate, they are easily eliminated.

When you play a backhand the face of the racket should meet the shuttle squarely and should continue to travel in the same direction as the shuttle for a short distance. The shot should feel crisp; the sound of the impact should also be crisp. But if you drop your shoulder during the stroke you will find that the face slides across the shuttle and feel and sound are both fuzzy. If you are playing a drive, the shuttle will rise more than you intended. The cure, of course, is to concentrate on keeping your shoulder level.

You may find, when playing drives, that the shuttle tends to go across court rather than straight. There are two possible causes. One is that the swing started too early and the face of the racket thus reached the part of the swing at which it faces across court when it hit the shuttle. The other is that the racket was not following through in the direction in which the shuttle was to travel. Again the answer is obvious—adjust the swing a little and see what happens.

The follow-through of powerful or fairly powerful strokes in badminton tends to bring the player back to the base position. If this does not happen after a backhand drive or clear (when you are not playing the shots at full stretch or in desperation) there are several possible faults. It may be that you are reaching the shuttle late (poor or slow footwork) and therefore having to play the shuttle after it has passed you. You may be late in playing the stroke because you have not prepared as you moved towards the shuttle—take the racket with you as you turn. You may not be anchoring yourself before you hit the shuttle; for instance you should have your right foot on the floor before you hit the shuttle. If the weakness is in the overhead clear, it probably means that you are not playing into the shuttle (i.e. moving towards the net as you play the stroke). Ideally for the backhand clear you should be waiting so that a shuttle dropping vertically from a clear would drop onto your right shoulder. The last possibility is that you are trying to hit the shuttle too hard, using too much body swing, and thus losing your balance.

If you find that you are having difficulty in getting your right foot across when playing a drive, because the rally is too fast, try turning your body only, while stepping to the left with your left foot. You should be able to get all the force you need for most drives with this swing; you should also be able to recover more quickly.

Alternative Backhand Clear

You will see some good players, particularly ladies, clearing the shuttle from baseline to baseline on the backhand by hitting the shuttle upwards from about chest level. To do this they twist their bodies round to the left until they almost have their back to the net. Their feet are apart and facing the left side line. The shuttle is hit with the full power of their body and arm—and they hit it very hard. The forward swing will start with the racket at about elbow-level. From there it will travel upwards to hit the shuttle at about chest-level opposite the right shoulder and follow through upwards in the direction of the shuttle. It is vital that the face of the racket meets the shuttle squarely, therefore the shoulder must not drop during the swing. The follow-through should be long and free; it will turn you round to face the net and help you to return to your base.

There can be little doubt that the overhead backhand clear is the better stroke. It is equally clear that some players may never develop sufficient wrist strength to play it effectively. This clear at a lower level is an effective alternative, but it is very much a second best.

Conclusion

I hope that you are now convinced that the backhand is basically an easy stroke. If your wrist is not strong enough, a few minutes' exercise every day will rapidly develop its strength and hence the power of your stroke. You will then come to enjoy backhand strokes, and will look forward to rallies in which you can use the versatility and control inherent in all good backhands.

6

SERVICE

DO REMEMBER—you can score only when you are serving. Thus the ability to serve well is worth many points, regardless of the standard of play. Having delivered this warning I must do my best to help you to serve well.

There are three basic services: a low, short one; a high, long one; and a long one of medium height. Each has its uses. Quite obviously you will experiment in serving to people until you find the one that they like least. But, as a general rule, the low service is the basic service for doubles and the high, long one for singles. The chapters on tactics explain why this is so but in passing a brief explanation may be of interest. Most doubles games are won by the side which attacks most effectively. A high service, which may be smashed, presents the attack to your opponents. A low service, which should ideally travel downwards immediately after passing the net, gives your opponents less opportunity of gaining the attack and maintains the initiative for the serving side. In singles the players are sparring for the initiative. While the shuttle is vertically above the centre of the baseline, there is stalemate; neither side has the initiative. A low service, unless it is used with discretion, may give the receiver the chance of gaining the initiative with a variety of effective shots.

Figure 1 showed the difference between the courts into which service must be delivered in, singles and doubles. As in most ball games, service must be played diagonally into a specified area.

It is important that you know and understand the laws concerning service because several of them are broken inadvertently in both club and match play, which causes quite unnecessary bad feeling. Although these laws are in Appendix II, I am including them here for easy reference.

'It is a fault:

14 (a) If, in serving, the shuttle at the instant of being struck be higher than the server's waist, or if any part of the head of the racket, at the instant of striking the shuttle, be higher than any part of the server's hand holding the racket.

14 (b) If, in serving, the shuttle falls into the wrong service court (i.e. into the one not diagonally opposite to the server), or falls short of the short service line, or beyond the long service line, or outside the side boundary lines of the service court into which service is in order.

14 (c) If the server's feet are not in the service court from which service is at the time being in order, or if the feet of the player receiving the service are not in the service court diagonally opposite until the service is delivered. (*Vide* Law 16.)

14 (d) If before or during the delivery of the service any player makes preliminary feints or otherwise intentionally baulks his opponent.

14 (e) If either in service or play, the shuttle falls outside the boundaries of the court, or passes through or under the net, or fails to pass the net, or touches the roof or side walls, or the person or dress of a player. (A shuttle falling on a line shall be deemed to have fallen in the court or service court of which such line is a boundary.)

16. The server and the player served to must stand within the limits of their respective courts (as bounded by the short and long service, the centre, and side lines), and some part of both feet of these players must remain in contact with the ground in a stationary position until the service is delivered. A foot on or touching a line in the case of either the server or the receiver shall be held to be outside his service court. [*Vide* Law 14 (c).] The respective partners may take up any position, provided they do not unsight or otherwise obstruct an opponent.'

Law 14 (a) causes most of the trouble although the other laws also lead to dispute at times. The problem is that the server is often under nervous pressure, because he knows that the service will be killed unless it is a good one. Law 14 (a) requires him to serve upwards towards the net with the possibility that the shuttle will be still travelling upwards (and hence be easily killed) as it crosses the net. Anxiety causes the server to raise the point of impact to get a flatter trajectory until, unconsciously, he is producing a foul service. There are always some, of course, who may deliberately flout the Law, but I think that they are in the minority.

You will have noticed that there is no law about a 'let' service as there is in some ball games. If the shuttle touches the net as it passes over it, and is otherwise a good service, it is not a fault.

Low Service

The low service is the only stroke in the game for which a wrist movement is not recommended. Instead you should use a swing generated by body and arm movement to persuade the shuttle in a flat arc over the net, so that it would just reach the front service line if it were allowed to fall. There are so many individual methods of serving that I hesitate to specify a particular system, but recommend one I must. However, I am doing it on the assumption that readers will adapt it to suit their particular inclinations.

All good services that are based on a smooth swing instead of a wrist flick have one thing in common. During the six inches before impact and also immediately after impact the racket is *not* following a curved path. It is moving along an almost straight line and pushing the shuttle. Apart from the advantage of a flat trajectory, which is gained from the push, the movement of the racket allows a much larger margin of error. The principle is similar to a straight bat in cricket. This push should be incorporated into your swing.

Now let us consider the rest of the swing and the associated body movement. The feet are usually fore and aft, and may be a shoulder's width apart or quite close together, whatever feels comfortable. During the swing the weight moves from the back foot to the front one. The shoulders also turn during the swing because the upper body will be facing almost the right side line when the weight is on the back foot but the net at the moment of impact.

If you now follow the step-by-step instructions below you will add the arm swing to this body movement.

1. Stand facing the net with your feet a comfortable distance apart, fore and aft.

2. Take your racket in a forehand grip. Let your arm and racket hang straight down your right side.

3. Rest your right elbow on your hip and raise your forearm and racket a short distance sideways from your leg.

4. Turn your shoulders to face the right side line, letting your arm turn with it. The face of the racket should now be facing the side line. Your weight should have moved on to your back foot.

5. Now cock the wrist. (That is raise the racket a little keeping the face of the racket towards the side line.) The wrist must remain in this position during the whole of the swing.

6. During the forward swing the weight is transferred to the front foot and the upper body turns to face the net. The arm stays close to the side until the player is facing the net, when the arm swings forward in the direction the shuttle should travel.

Repeat the swing several times until it feels relaxed and natural.

The shuttle should be dropped vertically from shoulder-level to fall about twelve inches in front, and a little to the right, of your front foot. If the swing I have just described is used and the shuttle dropped accurately it has been calculated mathematically, I believe, that a good service will be produced. My experience confirms the efficiency of this method.

The swing I have described is suitable for a service from two to three feet behind the front service line; this is the position from which many men serve in doubles. In ladies' and mixed doubles, the ladies often serve very close to the front service line and considerably shorten the swing. The shoulders turn very little. The elbow is bent more, but the wrist angle remains the same. There is very little transfer of weight because the feet are close together during the stroke, but the weight is forward, over the shuttle, at the moment of impact. If you shorten the swing, you must reduce the height from which you drop the shuttle. Trial and error is the only means of establishing the height that suits the swing you develop.

A good low service is seldom acquired without practice, which may be obtained during a game or off the court. The essentials are a smooth unhurried swing which will control the shuttle as it glides over the net. The stroke is gentle, almost a caress, rather than a hit.

One final bit of advice. Watch as many good players as you can and try to get the *feel* of their service. Note that they never hurry, neither do they keep their opponents waiting unnecessarily. Their swing appears to be grooved and its appearance does not vary however many low services they play. This is the ultimate objective: to find a method which enables you to serve well, to practise it until it becomes ingrained and to repeat it on demand.

Notes

Do try to get a flat trajectory even if the shuttle goes into the net to begin with. If the shuttle always goes too high, check—are you hitting it too hard (i.e. would the shuttle land a foot or more beyond the opposite service line); are you keeping your wrist cocked; is your weight moving forward onto the front foot?

If it always goes into the net, check—is the wrist cocked too far; is the weight moving too far forward; is the point of impact too low; are you hitting the shuttle too gently?

High Service

The faults are the same as in the low service. The most common one is moving the feet before the shuttle is struck. This stroke is very different from the low service. You must use a full swing, you must make full use of your wrist, and you must hit the shuttle high and deep to the back of the service court. Remember that in singles this is 2 ft. 6 ins. deeper than in doubles. The start is similar to the low service in that you should stand with your feet about a shoulder's width apart; they should point towards the net and the shoulders should be turned so that the chest faces the right side line. Then proceed as follows:

1. Take the racket in a forehand grip. Swing the right arm back until it is at shoulder-level and it forms a straight line with the shoulders.

2. Swing the arm like a pendulum until it reaches shoulder-level in front of you. Keep the arm straight.

(*Note*. The swing should have turned the shoulders so that the right shoulder now points towards the net and the chest faces the left-hand net post.)

3. Repeat this pendulum swing but start with the weight on the back foot and then transfer it to the front foot as you swing.

4. Now, instead of swinging the arm straight back, bend the elbow and cock the wrist as the arm moves backward, and stop the backward movement when the upper-arm is about forty-five degrees to the vertical. At this stage the elbow should be pointing toward the ground and the head of the racket should be close to the right shoulder.

5. You will find that the left arm tends to come up in front of you in sympathy; let it, it helps to balance the swing.

6. Now swing your arm and racket forward with an under-arm throwing action.

The harder you swing, the further your arm will want to follow through and your right foot will be dragged forward more quickly, hence the risk of a fault.

Now the shuttle. Hold it in the same way as you did for the low service, drop it in the same way; you will find that the swing will automatically drive the shuttle high into the air. Practice is all that you need to obtain accuracy.

If the trajectory is too steep, so that the shuttle goes high enough but falls well short of the back service line, check the following points. Is the shuttle being struck when it is too high? It should be between knee and waist-level when the racket hits it. Is it being played too close to the body? It should be about twelve inches in front and a little to the right of your left foot. Is the follow-through too vertical? The racket should travel along the same path as the shuttle for a short distance after impact. Has the weight remained on the back foot? This alters the whole shape of the swing immediately before and after impact with the result that the racket face is travelling almost vertically.

If the shuttle trajectory is flat, the shuttle may again be too close to you, or the wrist not cocked far enough on the back-swing, or you may be using the wrist too late on the forward swing.

If the shuttle is not flying far enough, the swing may be too short, or the wrist not being used enough; alternatively, the wrist may not be effective because the shuttle is dropped too close to the body. But it may be that you haven't got the knack yet or that you haven't developed enough strength.

Drive and Flick Services

This is an alternative to the low service, to be used against someone rushing it or getting you into difficulties by returning your low service very effectively. At other times it may be used to upset opponents, particularly if you can serve it very accurately and if they have difficulty in dealing with a particular variation.

The stroke is played in the same way as the low service until immediately before impact when the wrist is flicked through, driving the shuttle quickly above the reach of the opponent to the back of the service court. Alternatively it may be driven to pass the opponent at about head-level so that he is forced to play a most awkward shot behind his head. Obviously surprise is extremely important, therefore the preparatory actions must be identical to the low service. It is also important that the shuttle does travel quickly, otherwise the receiver will be able to step or lean back and play an effective return.

The direction is also important. Obviously if you play the flat drive service towards the forehand, your opponent should have little difficulty in dealing with it. If, however, it is on his backhand side, it is unlikely that he will be quick enough to play the shuttle while it is in front of him. How quickly he gets back to it depends on the quality of the service and on the speed of his reactions. It is difficult to play this stroke against a player in the left court unless he stands well out of position (i.e. towards the centre line). Conversely, the closer the player stands to the service line in the right court the less space there is to play the drive into.

The alternative, higher, flick service is often best played towards the farthest corner of the service court because this gives the shuttle more chance of getting beyond the reach of the receiver.

The services, as these paragraphs will have indicated, are not merely a means of starting a rally. The server should use them to gain as much legitimate advantage as possible. Each time you serve to an opponent, take stock of the situation. Is he standing in the same position; has anything changed about his readiness to move; is he holding the racket in the same position? When you serve to him try to note his reactions. Does he seem to be on his way to the net almost before you have struck the shuttle? Is his first reaction to lean back as if to receive a flick service? Does he wait for the shuttle to come to him? Does he habitually return the service on his forehand, his backhand or with a pan-handle grip? Does he favour services to particular parts of the net (e.g. slightly to his right)? Has he any habitual returns that you might be able to anticipate and turn to your advantage?

Answers to these questions can help you to decide how best to serve to an opponent. The better his standard, the fewer weaknesses there will be in his play. You will have to rely more and more on the accuracy of your service. By accuracy, I mean your ability to keep the shuttle very low and in a flat trajectory as it crosses the net. You will also need to try to anticipate the return. But some players are extremely deceptive when returning service, so much so that any attempt to anticipate the return is certain to lead to difficulty. One must steel oneself not to move until he has struck the shuttle.

10 1 Position for server in men's and ladies' doubles and also for the lady serving in mixed doubles
  2 Position for server in men's and ladies' singles and also for the man in mixed doubles
  3 Position for server in men's and ladies' if a side's formation is adopted

Figure 10 shows the various positions for serving. The man in mixed doubles remains in the centre of the court after serving because that is his base of operations. The lady in mixed, and men or ladies in doubles, usually need to follow their services into the net (i.e. to a position on or in front of the service line). This movement must be made immediately the shuttle has been struck. If you have served to the outside of the court you must follow the line of the shuttle in moving forward to your base. Having moved, the server is now ready to deal with net shots and is also out of his partner's way. It is a very good idea to have your racket up as you go in to deal with any soft shots pushed close to your body. But resist the temptation to snatch at fast shots unless you feel confident about dealing with them effectively. Of course you may, by arrangement with your partner, practise them during club games, but eliminate them from matches until you are sure of your ability.

If you serve a flick service, you must decide whether to move towards the net or remain farther back. If your service has been very effective and the opponent seems unlikely to be able to play an attacking shot, you must be prepared for a drop-shot and should move in to the net. If his reactions have been quick enough and he is in a position to attack the shuttle, your reactions will depend on the position of the shuttle, his methods of attack and your ability to defend. If the shuttle is high enough to permit him to play a smash, the cross-court return is your responsibility. It may be dealt with by moving in close to the net to take the shuttle at head-level or by moving back a little to take the return on the backhand (service from the right-hand court) or forehand (service from the left-hand court). If the reply to the service requires a round-the-head stroke, the shuttle will tend to have a flatter trajectory the lower it is played. This situation most often arises in reply to services down the centre from the right-hand court. The server can often deal with straight returns and those towards his forehand. If the receiver can be tempted to play a hard, flat return and you can sight it, early, you may reap a fine harvest of points. The better the player, of course, the more difficult it is to tempt him to play more than one.

If you do move back a little after serving your flick, you will leave a large gap all along the net. You must, if possible, be ready to deal with most shots to the net in addition to taking your share of attacking shots. Usually your partner will cope with those to the corner of the net farthest from you.

Some players change the base from which they are serving to try to gain advantages against some players. In theory there is no advantage to be gained, because the receiver simply changes his position also and adapts his strokes to the new situation. This theory works well when the players involved are experienced, confident and have a variety of strokes. But if one of these adjectives does not apply, the server has found a potential weakness to exploit.

The commonest alternative to serving from the centre in the right-hand court is to move to the tramlines. The shuttle may then be driven into the backhand corner of the service court or obliquely into the tramlines at the front of the service court. You will understand from these descriptions that I am talking about doubles. At certain standards, and particularly in mixed doubles, there are many players who cannot cope with this service. Until they develop a reliable reply the service should be used, particularly in matches. But it should not be used continuously because this will merely give your opponents plenty of practice and, although you may gain a psychological advantage as well as a score advantage, a time will come when their repeated attempts produce some form of reply. Save the service until you really need it, say 10– or 12–all in a fairly close set; the score should give an additional psychological advantage to the server.

Tall men sometimes stand close to the front service line, hold the shuttle out in front of them and then serve with a very short movement of the racket. Usually the movement is quick enough to drive the shuttle to the back of the court. The short, low service is played by checking the wrist. The receiver finds the shuttle over the net so quickly that his reaction is usually late, until he decides to move back a little to gain time. The initial advantage of surprise is usually cancelled by a retreat of six to twelve inches. But it does mean that the receiver will have to take the low service below net level which is very much to his disadvantage. Tall men and ladies should, therefore, try altering their service base until they find the one that gives the maximum advantage.

In both of these services—the drive from the tramlines and the flick from tall men—there is a risk of playing the shuttle above waist-level (which is a fault, of course), because the servers are straining to get a flatter and flatter trajectory into their services. If you use either of these services it is worthwhile asking someone to check your action.

I think it best to leave the high service in singles until the chapter on singles, but it will be obvious that some of the following comments about men's, ladies' and mixed doubles could also apply to singles.

Why are you using the high service in doubles? Because the ladies don't like it; they may not have strong overhead strokes? Because your defence is stronger than your attack? Because your opponents are beginning to mistime their overhead strokes? Because your opponents have dealt so effectively with low and flick services that you have only the high service left? These are the main reasons.

If you serve high to the centre of the court in men's and ladies' doubles you often put yourself in a very strong defensive position because of the wide range of defensive returns you may play. The closer the service goes to the side lines, the smaller the range of defensive shots become. These comments are made on the assumption that the attack is strong and the player at the net is effective.

If the attack is weak, serve to the outside edge of the court in the hope of taking the return early and either pushing it straight back or driving it across court past the player at the net. If the game is mixed doubles serve to the tramlines to give the lady a chance to pick off the cross-court return leaving the man to deal with the straight ones. A high service down the middle eliminates the lady from the game as far as attacking shots are concerned, leaving the man to deal with all the replies. This is dealt with more fully under 'Mixed Doubles'.

Do remember that the high service should be dropping vertically on to the back service line so as to give as little assistance as you can to your opponent. If the shuttle falls at an angle he will not be forced to the back of court and he will also take advantage of any pace there is on the shuttle.

Service is extremely important: you cannot win points except when you are serving: practice makes perfect: there is no real excuse for not practising.

7

RETURNS OF SERVICE

MOST REASONABLY, good badminton players have worked out, by a process of trial and error as well as of logical thought, where to stand when receiving service in singles or doubles. This chapter deals with the logic, leaving the trial and error to you.

Let's be clear about your objective as the receiver. In doubles you are determined that, if at all possible, you will win the rally with your return or else force your opponents to play a weak shot from which your side will win the rally. An excellent illustration of this was a doubles in the All England Championships between the Choongs of Malaya and Kobbero and Hammergaard-Hansen of Denmark. Both pairs in their earlier games of the Championships had dominated their opponents' services, and their meeting was expected to produce a tremendous struggle for dominance. The expected struggle took place; the Danes won. In fact their dominance was such that the Malayans had to resort to high services. The Danish pair's returns to low and flick services were quite brilliant and devastating.

It might be argued that if club games were approached in this spirit there would be few rallies and the games would be much less interesting. But in the doubles I mentioned, there were many thrilling rallies despite the number of services that were killed. You will also find that as the receiver becomes more efficient, so the server must improve. This leads to one of the most fascinating battles in the game.

In doubles, players should ideally wait to receive service close to the front service line: the positions are marked in figure 11. From this position it is fairly easy to attack a low service,

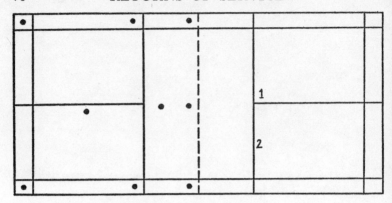

11 1 & 2 Positions for receiving service
The dots represent the areas to which returns of service
are usually made

but if the server produces an unexpected flick service, the receiver may not be able to get back quickly enough to return it effectively. For most players, therefore, a compromise must be reached: a position must be found which will permit the low service to be attacked and not let the flick service be a danger. But do recognize that such a compromise on the part of the receiver means that the server has won the first round in the mental battle. The farther back from the service line the receiver stands, the easier life becomes for the server.

In receiving service the movements will have to be basically forward or backward. They will have to be quick, indeed very quick. The feet need to be fore and aft like a runner at the start of a race and, like the runner, the knees should be bent ready to project the body forwards or backwards.

The body should be balanced with most of the weight over the front foot. The front leg should be bent at the knee so that it is ready to act as a spring. It is important that the spring be prepared, because the delay otherwise involved is sufficient to convert a service that could have been killed into one that has to be played upwards.

Ideally, the shuttle should be struck just as it crosses the net. To obtain some idea of the meaning of this, try standing at the net with your racket at net level. Get someone to serve towards your racket. Unless the service clips the net, you should find it quite easy to knock the shuttle steeply down on to the floor. The farther you move away from the net the more difficult it becomes to kill a reasonably good low service, unless you step into the net again. Thus any delay in moving forward to return the low service places the receiver under a disadvantage since the shuttle will be farther from the net and probably below net level when he strikes it.

Not only must you move forward quickly to the shuttle but you must reach forward at the same time. Try standing ready to receive service with your left foot on the front service line. Take one step forward and from there try to reach the net with your racket. You should find it quite easy to get close to, or even touch the net. One step and a stretch and you are in almost the ideal position to return a low straight service!

Now try moving backwards as if to receive an overhead flick. The trajectory of the flick means that you seldom, if ever, need to have your feet nearer than six feet to the back service line. Your reach will account for almost another three feet and the speed and trajectory of the shuttle will ensure that if you cannot hit it within about three feet of the back service line, it will fall outside the service court.

Ignoring the direction of the service, we have now reduced the receiver's movements to one step forward and two steps backwards. If he moves in the correct direction, i.e. forward or backwards, immediately the server strikes the shuttle, the receiver should be in a position to deal effectively with both low and flick services—provided he moves in the right direction! But how do you know which is the right direction?

Many people have habits or mannerisms which forecast what they are going to do. One girl I knew, who was a superb server, always bent her knee a little before her flick service. One man raised his right shoulder very slightly when serving low. It's too late to look for these signs when you are on the court; you need to study the server when you are sitting at the side. The simplest method I have found is to describe mentally the movements that I think I am seeing while he is serving. (I stress 'I think I am seeing', because our observational ability is usually poor and the first descriptions are almost bound to be wrong.) Start with feet and legs, then the body, arms, hands and racket and finally the head and face. With a little practice this becomes fairly easy, but you need to persist with your observations to begin with, because you can be sure that the very time you decide to watch a player he will seldom have an opportunity to serve, and when he does will play a high doubles service. You should also be selective. For instance, there is little point in studying the service action of someone whose service causes you no problems at all. Having identified what you think are the tell-tale actions you must test by forecasting the service before the shuttle is struck. Finally you must test it in a game.

If you know the signs that will forecast the service you should concentrate your attention on them. If you begin to wonder whether you will be able to recognize the signs or whether the server will have eliminated them, you are merely diverting your attention from the job in hand, with the consequence that your reactions are bound to be slower than usual. Clear any defeatist thoughts from your mind.

If there are no tell-tale signs then again you must concentrate your attention on the racket and the shuttle so that you can move immediately you distinguish which service is coming. The speed of the shuttle or the speed of the racket head will both tell you and they will both be in your line of vision. Some people are helped if they watch the shuttle closely, so closely that they see individual parts of the shuttle quite clearly. Others do not focus their eyes as closely as this. In both cases their reaction is very quick.

My own experience is that raising my eyes sharply to follow the faster flick seems to produce an immediate reaction, so that I am back and playing the shuttle without any conscious decision. Similarly, the slower pace of the low service seems to produce a reflex action which propels me towards the net. The only time this does not happen is when I try to think consciously about what the opponent is doing and my mind seems to take so long, comparatively speaking, to make a decision that I am always late in moving.

Most people have, literally, to project themselves backwards to take a flick that has passed beyond the reach of their rackets. Thus the shuttle will often be struck when it is behind the receiver. But if the flick service is short the receiver will catch up with it. A drive service may often be returned by a quick step backwards and a round-the-head stroke. If it is travelling too quickly for this, the server must again leap backwards to catch up with the shuttle.

If you habitually stand three feet back from the front service line to receive service, there is little point in reading this chapter and then standing close to the service line on the next club night. The result will almost certainly be very depressing. You must edge forward slowly, say six inches at a time, moving a further six inches only when you feel comfortable and confident at the current stage of the advance. You will find that your success will vary with the server, simply because some servers are so much more efficient than others. Therefore adjust your position according to the server, but against all of them keep edging forward. How close you get to the service line will depend on your reactions, your knowledge of your opponent's service and your confidence.

Do be confident. If a flick service catches you, say once in ten services, but you are handling the other nine effectively, your aggression must be paying its way. The odd success against you should not deter you.

There are recognized parts of the court to which returns of service may be played. But do not let those shown in figure 11 restrict your desire to experiment with others; it is not possible in the space available to cover all possible situations. To help guide your experiments the chapter also includes some generalizations against which you can test your ideas.

The places marked in figure 11 are gaps which arise in doubles when the service is low and the server moves forward towards the net. The returns to the net must obviously drop close to the net and, ideally, be well below net level before your opponent reaches them. This presupposes that the service has been taken early. The return to the tramlines just inside the service court must be travelling fast enough to get past the server and downward to ensure that it stays in the court. Again this presupposes that a low service has been taken early. The returns to the back of the court must pass both players by lifting the shuttle over their heads or driving it horizontally past them at about net level. The shots down the centre are usually aimed for the bodies of opponents. The one at the server is a fairly gentle push which appears, until the shuttle is hit, as if it was to be a very hard return. The deeper one to the partner must travel quickly so that he is forced to play a cramped, weak stroke.

While waiting to receive service, you will already have noted the gaps, if any, in the opponents' court. If you are human, you will at some time or other decide which gap to attack before the service is delivered and may then find that you have to deal with a service which cannot reasonably be put into the gap you had so carefully picked. The lesson, of course, is to deal with each service according to its merits. You will usually have very little time to judge the merits of a particular service and will develop habits because you will be faced with similar services over and over again. The habitual returns will almost eliminate the 'decision time' implicit in assessing the merits of a service and therefore enable you to play an earlier, more decisive stroke. But they will breed the danger that the opponent will learn your habits and be waiting for your return. It is desirable, then, to develop several different returns to the same service and use them according to the situation you are facing. It is quite surprising, once these various returns can be played without thought, how much time you do have to decide which gap to attack.

Not only should you have the facility to play alternative returns but you should also try to disguise them from your opponents. One of the easiest methods of doing this is to alter the direction of the face of the racket by a sharp twist of the wrist immediately before impact. Alternatively you may 'slice' the racket across the shuttle. Against some players you may feint to play the shuttle in one direction and in fact play it in another. All of these devices are useful provided they are used sensibly. But, if, for instance, a feint becomes an habitual stroke then the opponent will wait for it and it will lose its value.

Similar considerations apply to returns to flick services. If you get back quickly and catch up with the shuttle, you should have an easy kill to play because it will be equivalent to a mid-court smash. The gaps are similar to those already mentioned. Accuracy as well as pace is necessary for this return, because you are likely to be a little off-balance as you play the stroke and may be unable to recover to reach a well-directed return.

Some flick services can be taken very early, but in doing so you will often find that you have no time to take a back-swing and therefore cannot play a powerful stroke. This need not bother you because the pace of the service, plus a slight flick of your wrist will be all that is necessary to direct the shuttle down, steeply, over a corner of the net for an easy winner.

If the flick service is a good one, the accuracy of the return becomes pre-eminent. And the need to play the shuttle away from the opponent is also important, unless you decide to go for an all-out winner close to your opponent's body. The slower, accurate returns give you, the receiver, time to recover and prepare for any return. If you are well and truly caught, then the return must probably be defensive, in which case a straight clear to the back of the court is usually most successful. If you clear diagonally, the shuttle will have to travel farther (i.e. you will have had to strike it much harder).

A high service should be high enough and slow enough to permit you to get back in time to play an overhead stroke appropriate to the situation you are faced with. Briefly, you should attack if the opportunity is available (i.e. play a smash or a drop-shot) and play a clear only if this is really tactically desirable. The attacking drop-shot is usually more effective in mixed doubles than the floating one because it prevents the lady at the net from intercepting the shuttle. Because this attacking drop-shot may travel as far as the front service line it should be used carefully in men's and ladies' doubles. Ladies tend to move more slowly than men so that a floating drop-shot would be useful and effective in many ladies' doubles.

The return of a low service in singles must be mentioned because this service is being used more and more in good quality singles. There are four possible returns—one to each corner of the net and one to each back corner of the court. If any of these returns are within reach of the opponent before the shuttle reaches its target, the opponent may be able to gain control, if not win the rally outright. Obviously it will be difficult to get a low service to the centre away from an opponent; one to the outside opens up the court for the receiver. Singles players may develop the skill of playing the four basic returns with the same preparatory action so that the server will not know what return to expect until the last possible moment. This idea of 'holding' the stroke is basic to much of badminton. An Alternative is to lift the shuttle high and deep to the back of the court (i.e. return the low service with a 'high service'); this may be particularly useful in ladies' singles. But whatever you do, it is important to practise the possible returns so that you know you can play them accurately and consistently and then select the return appropriate to the situation you are faced with in a game.

Sometimes you will be faced by unorthodox services which may be upsetting until you get used to them. The commonest are services from extreme parts of the court (e.g. the tramlines), services that are played by tall men from directly in front of their white shorts, backhand services and services delivered by peculiar actions.

The services from extreme bases are easy to deal with provided you are reasonably confident of your ability to do so. The commonest is played from the right-hand tramlines, close to the front service line, to the nearest back corner of the service court. If played accurately, the shuttle should be at about head height when it reaches the receiver. Alternatively the server may drive the shuttle into the tramlines at the front of the service court. The receiver must stand in a position to deal with either of these services. The position adopted will depend

on the method of dealing with the service. But before considering how to play the shuttle do look at your opponents and decide
where the gaps are and therefore what shots are available to you.
Usually, immediately he serves, the server in the tramlines will
move a little to his left, parallel to the net, towards the centre
of the court. His partner will be farther back in the court and
a little to the left of the centre. There will be a gaping hole in
their defence at the corner of the net farthest away from the
server. There may also be a gap at the back of the court behind
the server; this will depend on the ability of your opponents.
There will be a small area near the middle of the net which may
tempt both opponents to go for the shuttle or both hang
back and leave it to the other. This area will vary from pair to
pair.

A gentle backhand stroke will be sufficient to play a drop-shot
to either of the gaps at the net against a service to the back of the
service court. A firmer stroke would drive the shuttle over the
head of the server into the forehand corner. Therefore the receiver may wait with the racket in a backhand grip, with the
elbow and wrist cocked and his arm raised ready to play either
a drop-shot or a drive/clear. Some people may find that they
need a little bit of backswing to play the shuttle to the back of
the court. To make things easier turn round to face the receiver
with the right foot slightly forward, close to the centre line. If
you stand about half-way between the front and rear service
lines you should find that you can also reach the alternative
service to the front service line fairly easily. Immediately you
have identified the direction of the service move towards the
shuttle. This is particularly important with the service to the
back of the court because you want to play the shuttle as high
and as early as possible to get it back over the net quickly and
give your opponents the least possible time to get to it.

If, however, you decide to play a round-the-head stroke
against this service, then you must wait in the same position but
with your chest parallel to the net and your left foot forward.
The deeper service should be taken by stepping to the left and
playing the shuttle as early as possible. If you can take the

shuttle fairly high and early, you can pick your spot and put the shuttle away.

To begin with you may not be able to play anything other than a drop-shot because of lack of power in your strokes, or perhaps lack of confidence. Your opponents will anticipate the stroke and cut it off as it crosses the net. If you return to first principles you will realize that you have achieved your first objective, to get the shuttle back over the net. So persist in playing returns to the net until, as a result of practice, you suddenly find the stroke is becoming easier and easier and your opponents are failing to win the point. This is certain to happen provided you do not let the server make you lose the little confidence with which you started. If you can practise with a friend, well and good.

The alternative service from the right tramlines to the front service line will almost certainly be below net level and some distance from the net when you reach it, therefore you will have to play it upwards. The possible returns are drop-shots to the net and high returns to the back corners of the court. A drop-shot has the obvious advantage that the shuttle should have fallen below net level before either opponent can reach it and should therefore be preferred to the clear.

The other unusual services I mentioned often need a temporary adjustment (i.e. a retreat of about a foot) if you find that they are causing you difficulty. But do begin to edge forward and regain any initiative that you may have lost.

Theoretically a server should be conscious that he is at a disadvantage when serving in doubles, because the service has to be played upwards. It is the function of the receiver to make the server aware of his disadvantage by being ready to move and by attacking the service at the first opportunity. If this competition between server and receiver ceased to exist, I am sure that badminton would have lost one of its most absorbing challenges.

8

NET PLAY

THE PRINCIPLE BEHIND most shots at the net is simple. The face of the racket must be at right angles to the direction in which you want the shuttle to go.

This is very easy to write, but in the heat of the game not so easy to do. Nor does it take into account the strength with which the shuttle should be struck. But having watched many hundreds of net players I have come to the conclusion that they have more control over the strength of the stroke than over the direction. Thus I am putting the emphasis, first of all, on direction. One very good net player once told me, 'Whenever the shuttle is travelling slowly enough I watch to make sure that it meets the racket squarely, but particularly I watch shots at the net because the margin of error there is so small.' Try bouncing a shuttle on your racket, watching to see exactly how the shuttle hits the strings. If you are like most people you will find that this is quite difficult, because usually players do not watch the shuttle closely enough or consciously enough. If you want to play good net shots you must be able to bounce the shuttle on your racket, controlling the direction and height of the bounce very accurately. As I have already said, I think you will find direction more difficult than strength.

When one comes to examine net play, a surprisingly large number of aspects need to be taken into account—the kill at the net against defensive or attacking shots, the delicate drop-shots used in net play, the footwork, the position of the player at the net, the function of the player at the net in doubles play. It might be useful to start with this last point and work our way backwards.

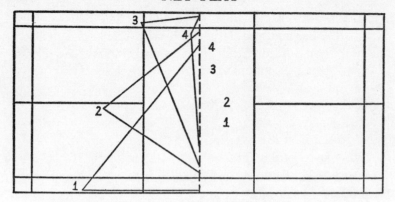

12 The lines show the possible angles of return of shots to
the net from points 1, 2, 3 and 4. The positions 1, 2, 3
and 4 show where the net player should stand to deal with
these returns. It is assumed that the shots to the net are
being played from below net level. The net player at
points 1, 2 and 3 would have to move backwards if the
opponent was playing the shuttle at about net level.
Players 1 and 3 would also have to move diagonally towards the centre of the court

Whether in men's, ladies' or mixed doubles, the function of
the player at the net is to limit the shots the opponents may
play with safety, to set up a kill for his or her partner, and to play
a winning stroke when the opportunity occurs. You can limit
the opponent's shots by placing yourself to cut off the widest
range of shots he could play to the net; position is all-important.
Figure 12 illustrates how the position of the net player varies
with the position of the shuttle in the opposite court. As you
can see, the shots to the corners of the net or one (not illustrated) well above the net player's head are the only strokes that
may be played without giving the net player a chance of winning
the rally. But the height of the shuttle and its distance from
the net also has significance. If the shuttle is well above net-
level and within reach of an opponent, the net player's influence
depends solely upon the distance the shuttle is from the net. If
it is close to the net, he has little influence because the shuttle
should travel past him too quickly for him to intercept it. If

it is at the back of the court, he should be able to cover all shots to the net and also deal with a cross-court smash. This situation should theoretically occur only in mixed doubles, but it will be an exceptional men's or ladies' doubles pair who do not find themselves defending in a front-and-back formation at one time or another.

While a player is at the net he must keep his racket up, so that the head is at least at face-level. His object—with few exceptions—is to strike the shuttle as it crosses the net. On most occasions this must mean that he is moving to meet the shuttle. Footwork is therefore very important.

Let's begin with one or two warnings about movement at the net. It is very easy in an exciting rally to get closer and closer to the net until your movements are suddenly restricted by the risk of touching it, which is a fault. Similarly, you may find in moving quickly across the net that your momentum takes you beyond the shuttle and you therefore cannot reach a possible cross-court return. If the shuttle is towards either end of the net, try never to get between the shuttle and the nearest post. A corollary of this is that you must try not to be drawn too far to either side. It is much better to develop the habit of reaching the shuttle with a step or two and a stretch, so that you are always able to recover to deal with a cross-court return. This is, of course, a counsel of perfection. But if you are absolutely on your toes, have your racket up and are really ready to move, it is surprising how many times the shuttle can be played by just a step and a reach.

The delicate shots are usually the delight of the ladies. Ideally the shuttle should be played at about the level of the tape and should topple over it to fall vertically close to the net on the other side. The lower the shuttle is at impact the more difficult it is to play the shot accurately, hence my emphasis on correct position and footwork. The grip is not particularly important for these shots, provided the racket is presented squarely to the shuttle.

If the net player is able to play the shuttle close to the net and above net level, it should be the end of the rally. The shuttle should reach the floor by the shortest route that will keep it out of the opponent's reach and inside the limits of the court. One of the most effective grips for these shots is the pan-handle, see figure 2 (c). If you hold your racket as if it were a frying-pan and then turn it over so that your hand is on top of the racket handle, you will have a pan-handle grip. With this grip you should be able to play shots in front of you from net-level on your left to net-level on your right. The base of the racket should bounce against the lower part of the palm and prevent you from hitting the net with the racket. With this grip you will be able to play strokes in front of you with very little preparation and with very little forward swing. Provided that you have remembered to keep your racket up, this should save time an important saving since there usually is less time to play strokes at the net than in any other part of the court.

If you do not at present play a variety of shots at the net, you may find that you need to practise them for some time, and may lose friends or partners in the process. To avoid this, start with the easy shots. Try to hit the shuttles that are not rising too quickly to the the net. The shuttle should be played downwards into the tramlines away from your opponents. Next try to kill those shots that are rising slightly more quickly. If you stand and wait for one that you can reach easily, you will seldom have a chance to play a stroke; do move towards the line of the shuttle all the time so that at least you have a chance of being there when the opportunity to finish the rally occurs.

As soon as you are reasonably proficient, introduce deception. Sometimes this may mean pretending to play a hard shot but in fact playing a soft one. If your opponents have reacted to the feint they will have little chance to recover in time to reach the shuttle. At other times you can disguise the direction, or change the apparent direction with a sudden twist of the wrist. As you become more competent you will find that you can handle faster and faster returns. As you try to develop your ability you will inevitably pass through periods when you are mistiming the faster ones, but if you persist you should succeed. However, do limit yourself to the ones you can strike in front of you, otherwise you will make life very difficult for your partner.

So far we have only considered those shots that are rising to the net. But a really competent net player should be able to deal with shuttles that are travelling flatly or even downwards. It requires a great deal of courage to start doing this but it is not nearly so difficult as it looks. The secret is to sight the shuttle as it is being struck by your opponent by looking at it past the head of your racket. Having the racket so close to your face means, of course, that you can use it as a protection if necessary. Once you have sighted the shuttle, it only needs a very slight forward and downward movement of your racket to put the shuttle on the floor. The timing is the only difficulty. To begin with you will tend to play the stroke too late, thus hitting the shuttle up into the air, but at this stage it is sufficient that you hit the shuttle at all. Control of direction will come fairly quickly if you persist. Do not be put off if you also find that you are playing the shuttle straight back to the person who struck it, despite your efforts to get it to the opposite side of the court. Almost certainly, the fault lies in changing the direction of the swing immediately after you have struck the shuttle and not just before impact. Timing, again, is the problem. The easy way to gain control is not to be too ambitious to begin with. Try just a slight change in direction. Then one day you will surprise yourself by playing a perfect shot into the tramlines away from your opponents. Thereafter nothing will hold you back.

Before leaving net play, we must have another look at what, tactically, you are trying to do and how you should set about it. The need to limit the strokes open to your opponents has already been mentioned. You may do this by careful positioning at the net, but you may also be able to force your opponents to play particular returns or tempt him or her to play habitual returns, particularly those that give you an advantage. The better the player, the more difficult this becomes of course, and there will be occasions when you have to fence for an opening by playing accurate straightforward returns until an opening appears.

Cross-court net shots look much more spectacular than straight ones and are easy to play once you have acquired the knack through practice. But they can be a snare for the unwary. The general rule is to avoid playing them until your opponent is out of position or off-balance. If you and your opponent are both at the net and to the right or left of the centre, try to play the shuttle towards the nearest tramline (away from your opponent); keep the shuttle close to the net. If you can play an effective stroke, your opponent may reply by a clear to the baseline, an accurate straight drop or a cross-court drop. The clear is your partner's; the drop-shots are yours. Follow the shuttle you have played, keeping your racket up, and maintaining a balance which will enable you to cover the straight or cross-court replies. The cross-court return should be dropped back or killed just as it crosses the net. If your opponent follows the shuttle to anticipate this straight drop you will almost certainly win the point by playing it at his body or past him. If his reply to your original stroke is a straight drop, you must again take it as it crosses the net and kill it or play a cross-court drop. The cross-court shot must travel close to the net otherwise the opposing player's partner may be able to reach it. Sometimes as you are about to play a straight drop-shot you will notice that your opponent has moved, perhaps very slightly, to anticipate it. You must try to be so balanced that you can immediately alter the stroke to a cross-court one if you want to. But, once you have started the stroke, finish it without alteration; indecision ruins many opportunities.

Once the shuttle gets close to the body, particularly at the net, it becomes very difficult to play strokes. Thus one of the ploys of net play is to force the shuttle close in to the opponent's body, and then wait, racket up, to gobble any return.

Another method of creating a winning situation is to play the simplest and most direct stroke and leave your opponents to try variations and thus to incur all the risks of making mistakes. This requires great concentration and agility because you will need to take the shuttle close to the tape and get it back below tape level before your opponent can reach it. In this way you maintain the pressure and may therefore force errors. But of course this method may become a habit; your opponents may be able to anticipate your returns and take advantage of them.

Occasionally your opponent will play a cross-court shot to get you into difficulty and you will be forced to take it well below net level. If your opponent is over-confident and follows the shuttle too enthusiastically along the net you may find that he has left a gaping hole into which you may play a cross-court reply. A sharp flick of the wrist is all that is needed, but the shuttle must travel quickly to win the point before your opponent can recover. How do you play this stroke? It depends on the situation, of course, but the principle is the same as for all net strokes—the racket must meet the shuttle squarely. Therefore, try swinging the racket without the shuttle to find out how best you can present a square face to the shuttle in the various situations in which you might find yourself.

Before leaving net shots we must look at the 'jab' which several good players are developing. As far as one can see, the result is that the shuttle spins, base over feathers as it crosses the net, and does not stop spinning until well below net-level. The stroke must be played close to the top of the net. The action is a jab straight towards the net with the racket almost horizontal. The head may be slightly below the level of the handle to produce the slight forward movement in the shuttle necessary to take it across the net. To begin with it is difficult to avoid hitting the net with the racket, but control may come with practice. If you can master the stroke, there is no doubt that you will have gained a considerable asset. But before you decide to spend any amount of time practising, stop, and think of priorities. How important is this one stroke compared with your need to practise others—service, backhand, accuracy in smashing, etc.?

Once you have some mastery of net play, it can become one of the delights of the game. To be successful you must have your racket up ready to play a stroke; you must try to anticipate your opponents' actions; but above all you must be determined that you will take all shots early and above net-level if at all possible.

9

SINGLES

ANYONE WHO ASPIRES to be anything of a badminton player should attempt to play singles. It will put him on his own, with the responsibility of covering a court 22 ft. by 17 ft.; face him with the necessity of playing clears that really travel the whole length of the court and test the accuracy of all his shots. This description ignores completely the physical, mental and moral pressures that the singles players must overcome. When played between good, evenly matched players, the game resembles chess: each move is balanced by a counter-movement aimed not only at maintaining the balance of power, but also at gaining the attack by probing for or taking advantage of slight weaknesses or small openings. The game demands patience and persistence as well as fitness, strength and stamina. Indeed, few other games are so physically demanding. Some players even claim that success in singles depends so much on strength and fitness that it is not a fair test of skill and, in consequence, is neither attractive nor interesting to play. It will be clear that I disagree with this opinion because it not only ignores the degree of tactical skill required to manœuvre an opponent out of position before a winning stroke may be played, but it also ignores the influence of strength and fitness in any sport that is physically demanding.

In this chapter the game is examined from various aspects—tactics, strokes, positional play and so on. Each needs to be dealt with separately, but in a game they are all intermingled. If a player has a weakness he can be assured that it will be shown up on the singles court because there are no means of hiding it. Hence all aspects are important.

Let's start with tactics. In all games of badminton a good method of analysis is to identify the gaps on the court: by these I mean the spaces a player must move to cover. The base of operations for a singles player is in the centre, or slightly in the front of the centre of the court. The gaps are, therefore, at the net, at the back of the court and down the sides. Our problem is to get the shuttle on to the floor in one of these gaps. We may do this by forcing our opponent so far out of position that he cannot recover in time. Or we may force him to play a weak return, which may be killed with a smash or an attacking shot at the net. Alternatively, ignoring the gaps altogether, we may make him lose the point by playing the shuttle into the net or out of the court.

The spaces at the front and back of the court are more obvious targets than the sides because the opponent has farther to go to get to them. To take advantage of the one at the back we must get the shuttle past him; the one at the front requires that we get the shuttle well below net level before he can reach it.

The opponent is likely to make errors when he is forced, by our anticipation and by the accuracy of returns, to play strokes more accurately than he is capable of doing consistently. Or he may be forced to play strokes of which he is not physically capable. He may also be hurried (and harried) or forced off-balance. He may become tired, lose concentration or lose confidence. Notice I have used the term 'forced'. Singles is not a negative game, but a game in which each player is striving to gain the initiative and this usually means securing an attacking position.

A shuttle dropping vertically on to the baseline or close to the net gives little advantage to the player who is to play the next stroke, provided his opponent is well-positioned and well-equipped to deal with other than extraordinarily good returns. If the shuttle is at any height between the front and back doubles service lines, a wide variety of shots may be played and, on most occasions, the receiver will be in dire trouble. Accuracy then becomes most important. Clears to the baseline must get into the tramlines, drop-shots must stay close to the net. If one relates this to service, it appears to mean that high, deep services are 'in' and low, short services are 'out'. Against an alert opponent who moves in quickly to take a low service early, this is indeed the case. But until you know how a player would deal with your low service, you cannot say that you should not use it against him. Similarly flick services may be tried, and drives that travel not too quickly into an opponent's body. The high service should not always have the same trajectory or be served to the same place. Obviously if you find a weakness in return of service you must try to exploit it. But you will only find such weakness by continuous exploration. If you can, for example, force a player to 'snatch' at a few inviting flick services and you win the points, he will usually be so annoyed with himself that the benefit gained exceed the points shown on the score card. The timing of these variations in service is extremely important. If you are having a run off one particular service, this is a good reason for not changing to another service. If your score is around 9 or 10 and one point is going to make a substantial difference you will be torn between attempting to gain a quick point or serving safely and playing for an opening during a rally. There are many other such situations to which unfortunately there is no specific answer. In each case circumstances must dictate the action you take: the steadiness and experience of your opponent; his (and your) tiredness; the pattern of the game up to that point, and so on. The best advice I can give is that you train yourself to weigh up the situation very quickly and arrive at a decision. Having decided what to do, do it. Do not let any uncertainty creep into your mind or your strokes.

The length of the high service is very important. If you find that you have little time to deal with returns from your service it is a sure sign that it is short. It is better to be, initially, an inch or two beyond the baseline. The direction is also important. One may generalize about it, but individual players have weaknesses or strength which may make generalizations untenable. The service down the centre narrows the possible angle of return. The ones to the outside open the angle a little and the server has to move a foot or so to the side towards which he has served, in order to cover the range of possible shots. The service to the corners permits the receiver to play straight shots down the side lines to the net or to the baseline; many players find these shots easy to play. It also means that a straight attacking clear does not need to travel too close to the server. On the other hand, some players are tempted to be too accurate in this situation; they want the shuttle to fall absolutely in the corner of the court. As often as not, it falls just outside. A similar situation occurs in the high service to the centre of the baseline. Some players revel in it, others are tempted into error. The better the player, of course, the less chance there is of gaining cheap points off service.

If we look at the situation from the point of view of the player receiving the service, we can consider strokes and situations that will also be relevant to many other parts of the game. A high service gives him three alternatives: to clear, to smash, or to play a drop-shot. Unless the service is short or the server has moved away from his base (unlikely in play of a reasonable standard), the smash is probably not useful at this stage. This leaves the clear and the drop. The action for both must be as nearly identical as possible, so that the opponent has to wait until the shuttle is struck before he can safely move to return it. A straight clear will require less effort but will not make the opponent move far; a diagonal clear will require extra effort but may make the opponent move farther, provided it is of good length. A high defensive clear will give the opponent time to get back to play a return; a flat attacking one will make him move more quickly but he may be able to play it early because it will be low enough to be hit before it reaches the baseline, otherwise it will fall out of court.

The drop-shots may be similarly analysed. A straight one has the shortest distance to travel, but the opponent also has the shortest distance to travel to get to it. It may, therefore, be returned more quickly which means that we also have to move more quickly to get to the return. The cross-court one is very tempting. It appears to move away from the opponent, it can probably be hit harder and the shuttle will therefore go faster. And somehow or other it seems much easier to keep the shuttle close to the net. But it may well be a delusion. The opponent appears to have farther to go to get to it but this is so only if you really are very accurate. The great danger is that you will not be sufficiently accurate and the opponent will get to the shuttle early enough to take advantage of the open court before you have time to cover it. So far then, stalemate on most shots, so what are you to do?

First make sure you know the shots—that you can play them well. Secondly, before you go onto the court, find out as much as you can about your opponent, preferably by watching him play singles. Try to identify his habits, strengths and weaknesses. Thirdly, work out a tentative strategy, i.e. one that you are going to test rather than use for the whole game.

The things to look for in an opponent may seem fairly obvious but are at times difficult to see. This may often be because we have no standards with which to compare them or because we have not learned to concentrate on a single player instead of the shuttle. So watch the player when he serves, tell yourself where he moves to immediately after the service. See whether he gets back behind the shuttle when it is cleared over his head or whether he is constantly having to stretch backwards. Try to assess how quickly he gets into the net for drop-shots and how well he defends against smashes. Try to distinguish lazy or careless habits. (Some players when going for a drop-shot run in close to the net when a step or so and a reach would have sufficed.) What happens after he has played a stroke? Does he immediately move back to base or to a part of the court in anticipation of certain returns, or does he stand and admire his handiwork before scampering to retrieve the next stroke. While you are doing this you should also be conscious of the direction of the return he is playing. In some games, players make charts to show the pattern of strokes and analyse these when deciding their strategy; you might consider doing the same.

Having absorbed some knowledge of the player's habits of movement, try to put them into their context: try to assess the pressure under which he is playing. This means watching the whole game for a time.

Lastly study the length and trajectory of his strokes. Make a determined effort to identify weaknesses in length, height or direction and relate these to the stroke that forced the weak return.

These last few paragraphs have outlined how to set about analysing a game, but do remember that they are an outline and you must complete the picture to suit your particular needs. The sequence in which you deal with the parts is not particularly important, but it is essential that you concentrate your whole attention periodically on the one player, despite all temptations to follow the shuttle or the game. In passing, it is worth noting that this detailed study will also teach you a great deal about the tactics of the game, particularly if you study very good players. You will then find, perhaps to your comfort, that they also have their weaknesses.

When you get on to the court against the opponent you have been studying, give yourself a margin of error in all the strokes you play until you have settled down. Use strokes that will make him reach for the shuttle, bearing in mind any strategy that you may have worked out. Use attacking strokes (the flat clear and half- or three-quarter speed smashes) when you are well positioned; play strokes to give yourself time to recover when you are under pressure. Do not try to get out of difficulties by going for startling winners because they do not usually pay dividends. Above all, be patient. If, for instance, you have observed that a series of attacking clears into the backhand corner will often produce a short return sooner or later, wait for the opportunity to make use of this information. Better still, try to pull your opponent towards the forehand side so that an opening into the backhand corner is made, then test your observation. If it proves to be correct you quickly acquire a bonus because, when he becomes conscious of the weakness, he may tend to guard it, thus leaving a gap for shots to the forehand. To some extent, this presupposes that you are able to control the game, which will not always be the case. Therefore you must also learn to adapt your game to the needs of the situation. This may mean either slowing the game down by playing shots that take the maximum time to reach their target (e.g. floating drop-shots or high deep clears), or making it fast and furious. You may prolong the rallies if you think his stamina is suspect, and so on. But do remember, the ability to adapt one's game to the situation is one of a good player and, like everything else, requires practice.

Sometimes your study of your opponent may confirm what you already know, that the player is much better than you are, and you may then be tempted to accept the inevitability of defeat. Whatever else you do, drive this thought as far away from you as you can. Most good players suffer unexpected defeats, so why shouldn't this be your turn to add to the number? First of all determine that you are going to try and try really hard. Next assess what you do best. Is your anticipation particularly good, have you lots of stamina or are your overhead strokes deceptive and accurate? Having made your assessment decide how best to use your assets. If, for instance, you have a natural flair for anticipation you must strive to analyse the pattern of play and to anticipate particular strokes so that you take advantage of any lack of accuracy or length in your opponent's play. You may take advantage of your stamina by trying to ensure that your opponent runs between strokes, that the rallies last a long time and that your opponent has no rest between rallies. If age is also on your side, you may find that you can tire your opponent by suddenly altering the pace of the game or by making him change direction frequently and suddenly. This leads, of course, to the use of deception, the third asset I mentioned.

The objective of your strategy is to make your opponent behave illogically. He probably expects to win. He may start off playing in a relaxed manner because of his confidence or he may play keenly to begin with and then ease off. Immediately he relaxes you must press as hard as you can. A good player will not be disturbed much if a few of his 'best' shots come back or if a rally that should have ended six strokes back is still going strong. But he is likely to become disturbed if this continues to happen. It is unlikely that he will be able to hide his concern from you. It will be evident in his increased alertness, in the more efficient manner in which he moves about the court. This is your first crisis. Can you maintain your pressure while he is struggling to regain the initiative? You must at all costs try to deprive him of time to think about what is happening, but you must not act unfairly. If one of his strokes hits the net and the shuttle is easily within your reach but on his side, go and get it and return to your service position without delay. Don't rush and tire yourself, but be business-like about it. If he wants to change the shuttle and you do not, think quickly whether agreeing to the change will give him as little rest as possible or whether maintaining what you think (i.e. that there is nothing wrong with the shuttle) will increase his tension. Look determined, act determinedly and concentrate as you have never concentrated before.

Quite often, in this situation, your next crisis comes with the end of the first game. Your opponent now has time to think; he now has an opportunity to start a game on level terms. If he is a really good player, it is unlikely that he will allow you any chance to gain the initiative during this game. But you must continue to concentrate and strive to find openings and opportunities to win points to put him off his stride or to gain control of the game. When the opportunities come, seize them and try to maintain control of the game for as long as you can.

If you are on the receiving end of these tactics you will almost certainly be able to look at the game in retrospect and decide what you should have done. The first point, of course, is that you should not have relaxed. The next is that you must ignore any excuses for your lapse that occur to you or that others suggest. The fact is that for a period your opponent was playing better badminton than you were. What matters is strengthening your game so that it is much less likely to happen again.

Some people do this almost unconsciously, others require a

conscious effort. I feel, however, that some who claim to do it unconsciously are merely looking for an excuse not to do it at all.

One final point about singles. Players are more likely to make mistakes if they must move to play a stroke. If they move about the court at an even pace they will become accustomed to this pace of movement and its effect upon strokes, and may settle into an efficient groove from which it may be difficult to dislodge them. Therefore, moving an opponent about the court is insufficient. You must make him change pace and direction; you must try to make him start late (by deceptive play) and, if possible, hurry him so that he plays strokes off-balance. Use the full width, but above all, use the depth. Watch singles matches and see how few players force their opponents on to the baseline. Be careful, however, that in trying to make your opponent run, you are not, in fact, running more yourself.

For those who are fit enough, have the strength and the mental and physical stamina, singles is an attractive game. Those not really equipped to play it should have a go because it is a short-cut to identifying deficiencies, and also a means of curing some of them because of the self-reliance it demands.

10

MIXED DOUBLES

IN THE MANY clubs I have visited, coached or played at, the game that seems most common is mixed doubles. To my mind it is the most attractive, in that it demands the accuracy of stroke play and the command of tactics typical of singles without the accompanying physical demands, and also permits the power strokes of men's doubles to be used. At its best, it provides the lady at the net with ample opportunity for delicate drop-shots, subtle feints, deceptions and sharp kills. It demands from her agility, speed and touch play. The men cover most of the court (which is as much as many want) setting up kills for their partners, or dealing with weak returns their partners have extracted from the opponents. They strive to work their opponents out of place by their control of pace, length, direction and trajectory. From the men, the game demands speed and stamina, power of stroke and at times a delicacy of touch to equal that of the lady at the net. How delightful it is to watch the cut and thrust of two good, evenly-matched pairs. But alas, how different it is in some clubs. The ladies stand at the net, slowly turning blue with cold, while the men bash the shuttle back and forth to each other. Then the men have the nerve to be annoyed when the ladies refuse to stay at the net! It could so easily be so different.

This chapter examines the principles of mixed doubles under three headings: the basic positions from which players should operate (including serving and receiving service), the tactics of the game, and defence. Each of these aspects is considered first from the lady's and then from the man's viewpoint. The chapter ends with matters that cannot be considered conveniently under these headings.

13 Serving and receiving service in mixed doubles
    1 Position of the men when serving. Ladies use their normal doubles serving position near the front, short service line
    2 Position of the lady while the man is serving
    3 & 4 Receiving service in the right and left hand courts, men and ladies
    3a & 4a Respective positions of lady while the man is receiving service in the right and left hand courts

It's best to start with the beginning of the game because, if the game starts off with the players well out of position, it is unlikely that they will be able to play an effective game of mixed doubles. The basic positions for serving and receiving services are shown in figure 13. These are not absolute positions which demand that you stand exactly on the cross. Rather are they indications of positions from which people find it easiest to cover the court. You may well find that you need to alter them by a foot or so, but if you find that you prefer to stand more than that away from them, weigh up carefully the pros and cons of your decision and adopt your method only when there is a clear advantage. For instance, serving from the right tramline to a lady's backhand is, at times, a sure method of winning a point. If the game really matters and the point matters go to the tramline and serve on to her backhand, because you win games by winning points, not by adhering to theories.

Ladies usually stand near the front service line to serve. Apart from service advantages, such as the short distance the shuttle has to travel across the net, it enables her to move her base of operations very quickly.[1] The lady moving forward after service must be prepared to deal with three shots: a return to the net, a diagonal push which she may be able to intercept or a straight push slow or quick. Ten years ago, at all but the highest standards, it was fairly easy to push the shuttle into or past the lady as she moved forward. But many are now copying the better players, and unless the push is played well it is liable to be intercepted by the lady. There are many ways in which she may do this. For instance, the smaller girls tend to hold their rackets as they would to kill the shuttle, at the net, when it is directly in front of them (i.e. the racket is vertical with the head at, or slightly above, face-level; the grip is sometimes shortened). In this way they are ready to play any stroke in front or to the side. Their knees are usually slightly bent and a shot lower than face-level is reached by bending the knees more. Shots below waist-level are usually returns from poor services to which the server usually has no reply. But some of these shots are pushed gently and the server often has time to play these, provided her grip is loose and she can get her feet and legs out of the way in time. The consequence is that the receiver has either to play the shuttle very accurately towards the tramlines, out of the reach of the server, play a shot that is too fast for the server to intercept, or play a good net shot.

There is the risk, of course, that the lady will be tempted to take shots pushed firmly past her into the tramlines, i.e. those she has to move backwards to reach or that she can only 'snatch'

---

[1] If the lady serves two or three feet back from the service line she is likely to be late in getting to the net returns. The object, remember, is to take these returns at net-level or higher *as they cross the net*; anything else is second best. The need to get to the net sometimes means that ladies who serve from a backward position have to move forward very quickly immediately they serve, and they often become susceptible to snatching at shuttles played into the tramlines. They also have little defence against shuttles pushed to their body. For these reasons I would recommend that ladies stand forward to serve.

at as they pass her. The 'snatch' usually cocks the shuttle up for the opponent to kill. Her partner can usually deal much more effectively with this type of return of service because he should be moving diagonally forwards. If you are to become an effective mixed doubles player you must learn which of these pushes you can take and which you must leave. The only method of finding out is by experiment. But do start with gentle, slow returns and then graduate to the quicker ones as your skill and confidence grow.

The lady will have similar returns to deal with when her partner is serving; but it is much easier for her when she is moving in along the line of her own service than when she has to step across into the line of her partner's service. Generally when the man is serving in good quality badminton the lady stands in front of her partner and a little to the left of the centre line, which reduces her difficulty considerably. If she adopts the alternative system of always being on the opposite of the centre line to her partner she or her partner is forced away from the centre line. This leaves many gaps on the court and provides the receiver with opportunities for a wide variety of returns. There is one weakness about the lady always standing to the left. When her partner is serving from the left, he must avoid angling the service too much to the right because this is asking for a straight net shot which his partner may have difficulty in getting. If, however, you have arranged this with your partner as a ploy against the opposing man she may be able to get to the shuttle quickly and flick it over his head to the back of the court. The ploy will not be effective unless it is used very infrequently.

During the rally, the lady must be ready at the net to deal with any shuttle that comes her way. Since the shuttle must be at least at net height when it comes into her court, she must try to keep her racket at that level. The time she will lose in raising it will often mean that she is too late to kill the shuttle above net level and will have to play a shot upwards and give the opponents a chance to play a winning stroke.

The lady must also constantly move across the net as the rally moves from side to side. If the shuttle is anywhere along the centre line in her opponent's court, she must be ready for a drop-shot to either corner, which means that she must be in the centre of the net. If the shuttle is close to the net, she too must be close to the net and almost opposite the shuttle— but not so close that she will hit the net if she moves. If the shuttle is farther into the opponent's court than the front service line, she must move back a little from the net; she will be on the base of operations when the shuttle is about mid-court. The advantage of being slightly further back is, of course, that the player is moving forward to meet returns whereas if she had stayed close to the net she would probably have had to move backwards and to the side to cut off well-angled strokes. The same principle applies if the shuttle is in the tramlines; but the net player must move her base a little towards the side where the shuttle is, to reduce the distance she has to travel for the straight (i.e. the quickest) return. Any cross-court returns should pass near her if they are hit hard, or be within a step and a reach if they are played less hard to the net. The exception is when she is on the defensive, when she must be on the side diagonally opposite the shuttle and back from the net in order to cut off cross-court smashes. The more strokes the net player can return effectively, the more pressure she can put on the opponents and the less they can put on her partner. Most ladies at the net seem to have an instinctive understanding of this but often have difficulty in developing their ability. This is understandable because there are few more exasperating things for the man than watching his partner make a mess of situations he is in a position to deal with quite easily. Thus ladies must use their discretion when developing their game and preferably seek sympathetic partners.

The golden rule of net play may be summarized very simply. If the net player can play a controlled stroke while the shuttle is in front of her or to her side and the stroke will not result in an advantage being given to the opponent, she should play the shuttle. The natural reaction of inexperienced players is, 'When do we have time to think so carefully about our strokes at the net?' One seldom does, of course. But when one can play the strokes without thinking and learn to recognize different situations quickly the decision to play or not play the shuttle is almost instantaneous. But even the best players make mistakes.

The lady must, of course, return all shuttles played to the net or those that are likely to land between the net and the front service line. Any that will travel farther into the court should be played only if she can strike them when the shuttle is in front of her and when she can hit them downwards. If she will have to move backwards or reach behind her, it is best to leave the shuttle to her partner. I clearly remember playing with a partner who came back suddenly for a shot I was moving forward to. Unfortunately I was lighter and bore evidence of the collision for several weeks.

Sometimes, in very good badminton, the lady stands about the middle of the court behind her partner while he is receiving service, which lets him go for the service without the restraint of having to get back for returns over his head. In adopting this formation the side assumes that the man will be able to force a fairly weak return if he does not kill the service. The lady is expected to finish the rally if a weak shot comes her way, while the man stays at the net. Sometimes, of course, this tactic does not work and the lady finds herself playing strokes under difficulties. What she then does depends very much on her strength and on that of the opposition. If both sides are evenly matched and the men have more powerful strokes than the ladies, she should try to get back to the net as quickly as possible. The ideal method is to play an attacking drop-shot straight down a side line into the tramlines and follow it into the net. The shot should be hard enough to get past the lady at the net, but not so hard that it is easily reached by the man. As she starts to move forward, she may need to call to her partner but this depends on the arrangements made beforehand. The advantage of this shot is that it maintains the attack while giving the lady time to get to the net. A particularly powerful lady player may decide that it is best to play out the whole rally with the man at the net. This is really a matter of discretion.

So far we have dealt mainly with position and readiness to
play strokes. We must now look at the tactics and fit returns
of service and net play, discussed elsewhere in the book, into the
game. It is quite impossible, of course, to cover every situation
and therefore I have confined myself to general principles which
may be applied in many situations.

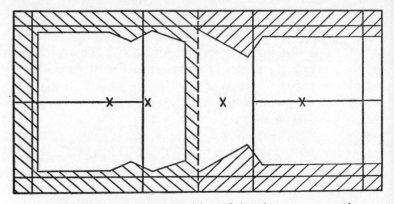

14 The x's represent the position of the players, man at the
    back and lady at the front. The hatched areas indicate the
    gaps which the players must move to protect and are the
    places into which the shuttle should be played
    The recommended position for the man is that shown
    on the right side of the net and, for the lady, that shown
    on the left

You will see from figure 14 that the openings on the court
are at the net in front of the lady, between the lady and the man
and behind the man. There are also gaps down the side. These
gaps will be opening and closing all the time, and since the
shuttle is usually played into gaps it is essential that you recognize them at each particular stage of the game. You must also
probe to establish which are the 'sensitive' gaps, i.e. those into
which your opponents do not like the shuttle to be played. In
addition you must develop the means of moving your opponents
so as to create new gaps or to enlarge existing gaps to such an
extent that the opponents cannot cover them.

In the following paragraphs the way in which the lady at the net can use this principle of moving opponents to create gaps is described. Much of what is written can be adapted by the man to help him control the game.

The first strokes of a tally may give no advantage to either side but you must, at the first opportunity, play a stroke that will really stretch your opponent. This is usually done by playing the shuttle as 'far' away from him as possible. I have put far in quotes because it must not be interpreted literally. If, for instance, you take the shuttle fairly early at the net, close to the tramlines on the left of the court and find that you are unable to kill it, you will often realize that both opponents have followed the shuttle across. Neither are likely to be quite as far across as you are. The farthest the man has to travel is across court to his left but this, in fact, is a fairly easy stroke for him to cope with, provided he has his wits about him and any speed about court. The shuttle flies fairly far, the man has far to run, but while he is accelerating the shuttle is slowing down and he is quite likely (almost certain) to reach it—once he knows you can play the stroke. When he reaches it, he has such a wide variety of possible returns that there is no space to consider them here. Any shots over his head are likely to be dealt with severely. This leaves a push shot into the nearest tramlines to a place near the front service line. The shuttle will take very little time to get there whereas he will have little time to get to it, and you will be in position to deal with returns to the net. If he has to stretch for it, it is most likely that he will play a clear to give himself time to recover. In this case your partner must carry on with the good work. But if he does play a stroke to the net you've got him! He will have to move back immediately towards the centre of the court so as not to leave too big a gap on his backhand. If you get to the shuttle early enough you can either repeat the dose until he makes a mistake (e.g. plays a loose shot) or does not move back towards the centre. But it is much better if you can learn to 'hold' your shot until he feels compelled to move, and then flick the shuttle into an appropriate gap. 'Holding' the shot is difficult to describe. It involves playing a normal swing with the body and

arm but holding back the wrist movement until the last possible
moment when you will decide the speed, trajectory and direction of the shuttle. This is most easily done when the shuttle
is travelling slowly and the preparation can be slow. The other
requirement, of course, is that it should be possible to play
several different strokes from the position in which you are
playing the shuttle. In addition to moving the body and arm
into the shuttle you may also begin to uncock the wrist slowly.
The unmistakable impression of a careful, gentle shot in a particular direction seems to hypnotize many players into anticipating it. At the last second the wrist can whip the shuttle in
an unexpected direction. The alternative, and equally effective
stroke, is to feint to play a very hard attacking shot and in
fact play a gentle one. There are many who seem unable to
control their reactions and who lean back in anticipation of the
hard shot.

There often appear to be enormous gaps at the back of the
court into which the shuttle may be played past your opponents.
In practice most of these gaps are a snare and a delusion. A
shuttle is effectively behind a player only when he is forced to
play the shuttle after it has passed him and he is then limited
in his variety of strokes. Thus clearing a shuttle over the head
of a man who is not out of position is merely giving him a
chance to win the rally. You must draw him forward and then
put it over his head or past him to the back of the court.
Alternatively you may lead him to expect a return to which he
will have to come forward, and then flick the shuttle over his
head.

It will help, perhaps, if I illustrate the application of these
principles to another situation. Let's take the deep backhand
corner as our target.

Few men have a really strong backhand; some have no effective alternative; many others have learned to cover the gap by
using round-the-head strokes. If your opponent has no effective
stroke deep on the backhand, you must obviously go for that
corner whenever you really need a point. But continually playing on this weakness in friendly games will merely ensure that

the games do not last long and that no one gets much pleasure out of them. If your opponent has a good range of round-the-head strokes but a poor backhand, then you must draw him well forward or across to his right before you can force him to use his backhand. If he has a really good backhand you have two strategies. It is unlikely that he will be able to play a backhand smash from near the back of the court; his returns will be an attacking drop-shot or a clear. Thus you may be able to take advantage of him by forcing him to clear, which puts you on the attack, or by anticipating his attacking drop. Be wary that he has not a cross-court one in his arsenal. This type of player will almost certainly have good round-the-head strokes so he also must be drawn forward or across the court before you can play the shuttle deep to his backhand.

If you do get the shuttle into the corner and force your opponent to play a backhand, you must be ready to capitalize on the situation. You should know the shots your friends are likely to play and be ready to kill any that present the least opportunity. You will have to be a little more wary with people you do not know. But the lady at the net has only two shots to watch for, a straight or a cross-court drop. She must be on her toes with racket up, ready to go for either, and must move as soon as she senses the direction of the shuttle. It is worthwhile taking a chance (if the score permits it) by counting on the straight one. But keep a check on your percentages of successes. If your guess is right and you are killing five out of six, you can afford to give your opponent the satisfaction of winning the odd point with his cross-court stroke. After all you will probably have the satisfaction of winning the game. But if half the returns are straight and half are cross-court, you must be reasonably certain of the direction before you move.

You will almost certainly come across the man who has the skill to return the shuttle at varying speeds very low over the net, and although the situation looks tempting, you realize as you go for the stroke that you cannot kill the shuttle. Often one muffs this stroke. Partly this is due to indecision, partly to deciding one's stroke too far in advance. If the shuttle is rising to the net, there should be no difficulty, provided it is not hit too hard. The shuttle must be struck crisply and the follow-through be negligible. The shuttle travelling horizontally or downwards presents the real problem, because our normal stroke will simply knock it into the net. This is because the base of the shuttle will swing downwards when we hit it. Returns in this situation must be very gentle if they are played close to the net; the base must be hit before the feathers cross the net. 'hit' is not a good word here, it suggests too much force. 'touched' or 'caressed' would be better, because if any pace is generated the base will turn downwards and hit the net. Be careful that you do play a stroke as required by the laws of the game; it is not sufficient to let the shuttle bounce off your racket. The alternative is to play a 'topspin' stroke, rather like a topspin drive in table-tennis. The racket is brushed upwards and forwards across the base of the shuttle, making it turn over quickly. If the stroke is played firmly the shuttle is given a downward trajectory after it crosses the net. Practice is necessary, of course, but this can be a very useful stroke.

This gives some idea of the means the ladies have at their disposal to make life interesting for opposing men. Play against the lady at the net is fully covered in the chapter on net play, but it may help if the principles are mentioned here. Kill any shuttles that may be taken above net level. Play the shuttle away from your opponent but not across in front of her and follow the shuttle to and fro along the net. Do not get closer to the side line than the shuttle. If you are a better net player than your opponent, make life difficult for her by playing accurate shots close to the net and deal ruthlessly with any weak returns. If you are evenly matched, play the simple straight-forward shot; let your opponent take the risk unless your best shots are the risky ones. If your opponent is better than you are, play net shots against her at times in friendly games to develop your ability, but in games that really matter keep the shuttle well away from her.

The man's base of operations is near the centre of the court. Ideally he wants to get on to this base immediately he serves, so that he is in a position to cover returns to any part of his court. If the man serves from the position he would normally adopt in men's doubles, he is going to have difficulty in getting back for returns flicked over his head. To avoid this, many players step backwards immediately they strike the service and astute receivers take advantage of this situation to return the shuttle while the server is still moving backwards. Apart from positional advantages, the person who serves from farther back can play a very flat service. But there are disadvantages. The shuttle will take longer to reach the net, giving the receiver more time to play his return. A flick service is less likely to succeed for a similar reason. But, in practice, the balance of advantage is usually with the service position shown in the figure.

There is a tremendous advantage in being able to play the shuttle shortly after it has crossed the net. Thus in good mixed doubles the man tends to come as far forward as he dares. It is quite devastating to play against a man who is hitting your drives just as they cross his front service line. It gives no time for recovery and one has to rely entirely on one's reactions to get the shuttle back somehow or other. Many years of coaching have convinced me that men of average standard tend to play much too far back in the court. They develop lots of ability to deal with the shuttle in front of them, but tend to be slow in getting back for shots played over their heads. If they would practise the latter, they would find their effectiveness increased considerably because they could then afford to move their base of operation two feet or so forward.

In some ways the man has a slightly easier job than the lady, but in others it is more difficult. The difficulty arises because the shuttle has farther to travel after he hits it and any flat or upward shots he plays may be intercepted more easily. But essentially he is trying to do the same as the lady at the net. A typical situation will illustrate this.

Let us assume that the shuttle has been pushed into the tram-lines on his right-hand side and he has reached it just above floor-level and just inside the service court. If he is very late there is little alternative to clearing the shuttle straight, high and deep to the back of the court. If he is well-balanced, he has a variety of shots, depending on the position of the opponents. If we assume they are not out of position he has little alternative but to push the shuttle low over the net to a similar position on the other court. The shuttle must be played firmly enough to get past the lady at the net but not so hard that it will travel deep into the opposing court. If it is played hard enough to reach say, mid-court, his opponent should be able to take the shuttle only a little below net level and has thus gained the initiative because he can play a wide range of shots with safety.

As soon as he plays the shot, the player must move back towards his base, otherwise he will leave his backhand wide open to attack. At a high standard, the men might play the shuttle back and forward, along much the same path, several times. Each is hoping that a lady will commit herself to intercept the next stroke, in which case he will play a cross-court drop-shot or put it closer to the side line than the previous strokes in the hope of forcing her to try an impossible shot. Alternatively, by altering the pace and length of the stroke he is hoping that the opposing man will return a loose stroke to the net. He may also be trying to cause his opponent to lift the shuttle diagonally cross-court towards the backhand corner. This is a fairly easy shot to cut off either by a backhand drop or a smash into the opposite tramlines; if the shuttle is fairly deep into the court before it is reached, it may be returned to the place from which it came—almost certainly the opponents will be moving rapidly across court at this juncture to organize their defence.

Another typical situation is a rally inviting drives of varying pace and direction. If you want to win a driving rally you must assume that your opponent will be able to return most of your drives and that something other than a big bang down the side line will be required. That 'something', by the way, is not a cross-court drive—unless your opponent is out of position and you are reasonably sure the lady at the net will not intercept it. A player is likely to play a bad drive if he is forced to stretch, if he has to play a cramped stroke, if he is late in playing the stroke. Our problem is to use one of these 'weaknesses' to gain an advantage. The easiest way to describe this is to play an imaginary rally from our forehand straight down the line on to his backhand. Let us assume that the shuttle is on our side, about mid-court on our forehand and a little below net-level. The first thing to remember is that we must not hit the shuttle so hard that it will still be rising when it reaches our opponent, but it must be travelling quickly enough to get past the lady at the net and still be travelling quickly enough when it reaches the man to limit the time he has to play it. If we return the shuttle into the tramlines, the reply is likely to travel back along the same line, so be ready for it, but also be prepared to move cross-court or to the back of the court if he plays another stroke. If the return is a drive, try to take the shuttle early, particularly if you can reach it while it is still above net-level. This is not usually possible, but quite often you can get to the shuttle when it is at net-level. You can now hit it harder. If the opponent has recovered quickly he will be back on his base by now, in which case you can try driving it hard past him down the side line. If he has not quite recovered, you have two alternatives. You can try driving the shuttle past him or you can drive it into his body, aiming for his waist. Assume that he is going to get the shuttle back, because if you succeed in making him play a weak return you or your partner will have to move in quickly to kill the shuttle. The principle is to keep the shuttle below net-level on your opponents' side by controlling the pace of the stroke, until you get a return above net-level which you can then play downwards or horizontally with greater force.

You may find that your opponent often plays his drives too hard and that they are still rising when they reach you. If you can get to these before they have passed you, you can play a wide range of downward shots, many of which are potential point winners.

If your opponent clears the shuttle, your first need is to get behind the shuttle and assess how far back in the court it is. If it is not in the back tramlines, you will usually smash. Remember that you have a partner. Whether direction or pace is most important will depend on the ability of your opponent, but because of the weak defensive situation in mixed doubles, direction is usually very important. Try a straight smash into the tramlines first and see what happens. Be sure to move forward as you follow through in case he plays a short straight return back along the tramlines. The harder you play this smash the less likely are you to get it accurately into the tramlines and the deeper it is likely to go into court. If your opponent cannot get to the shuttle quickly, this hard smash may create no difficulties for you. But if he can you have presented him with an easier shot to return than one that is almost at floor-level. If you aim at him, you will often find that he likes the shuttle at knee-level or lower but has more difficulty if he has to play a cramped stroke through the shuttle being aimed at his waist. What you must not do in this situation is play a clear, unless it is an attacking one calculated to catch your opponent off-guard because he is so obviously waiting for a smash.

If the shuttle is too deep for you to smash, you must still think about maintaining the attack if at all possible. Try an accurate straight half-pace smash or an attacking drop-shot and follow it in towards your base. You may well have to come back for another clear over your head, but if you do not go forward you will leave an enormous gap between you and your partner which your opponent will not be able to resist, however kind-hearted he may be.

I have assumed, so far, that your lady opponent is capable of cutting-off cross-court smashes. If she is, the only time when you are likely to play an effective cross-court smash is either against a short, high return, when you will beat her by pace, or when the shuttle is short and towards the right when you may be able to get it 'behind' her. This latter situation is one that many men try to create. Whatever the height of the shuttle, you can get it past most ladies provided you can get a return well to the right. Whether you play this particular stroke depends on the position of the man.

If the lady cannot cut off cross-court strokes you are in

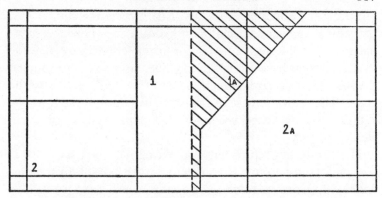

15 Triangle of defence. The lady at 1A is protecting the hatched area, her partner, 2A, is responsible for the rest of the court. The lady at 1 is ready to deal with returns to the net and also with cross-court returns from the man

clover, provided, of course, your partner is not in the same boat. The principle, of course, is to play cross-court when the man is unlikely to be able to intercept it.

Defence is best if it can be based on the triangle illustrated in figure 15. Under this system the man has to cover the un-shaded part and may also have to cover the straight drop-shots to the net if his partner cannot do so. This demands quite a lot from the man, but it also makes considerable demands on the lady because he is requiring her to play a fairly difficult stroke and one that he might not be able to play himself. The lady wants to get the shuttle onto the floor. How to do this against a smash has already been considered in the chapter on net play. If, in addition to cutting off cross-court strokes, she also de-cides to deal with straight drop-shots, she must be quite clear that she wants to get the attack which means playing a drop-shot or a half-court return. The one thing she must not do is whack the shuttle up into the air so that her opponent can have another try. After all, he might be successful the second time. The man also wants to get on the attack, which means playing similar returns. If the smash is flat he has a much wider variety of returns. In particular he now has a chance of attacking the attacker, especially if he can get the shuttle past the lady at the net. Attacking in this case does not necessarily mean hitting the shuttle hard. For example, you may play the shuttle straight back along the tramline, fast enough to get past the lady, but not hard enough to drive the shuttle deep into the court. The critical factor in this straight return is the time the shuttle takes to reach the floor. Off a flat smash, the time should be very short.

The cross-court return must be played hard and the angle is particularly important. If you can get the shuttle into the diagonally opposite tramlines, the opponent will have great difficulty in getting to it and playing an effective return. If the angle is less sharp and the shuttle lands about mid-court, he will rarely not get to it in time. Of course there are disadvantages in cross-courting. You take the risk that the lady will intercept the shuttle or that the man will get to the shuttle early. Immediately you play the stroke you must move diagonally back to your base in readiness for a return (assuming that the lady has not intercepted your stroke). It is interesting to note that the straight return effectively eliminates the lady and results in your moving a shorter distance than the cross-court does. But if it becomes an habitual return, you can be sure that it will be to your disadvantage sooner or later.

Some pairs find they are much better defending against smashes from a particular side, and, if forced on to the defensive, tend to clear so that the man has to smash against their strongest defence. In this connection it is interesting to note that the route past the lady is different, depending on the side from which you are attacking and assuming that the lady does not retreat beyond the service line. You will realize what I mean if you recognize that the shuttle must go past the net player's left shoulder (unless she is left-handed) if the smasher hopes to win the point.

What happens if the net player does retreat and you find yourself smashing against a sides pair, with each partner defending a half of the court? Obviously you are going to attack the lady (on the assumption that she is the weaker player). The gaps are similar to those in singles—at the net or at the back of the court. But you have a partner at the net and need not be as circumspect in your smashing as you would be in singles. You now start to play singles against the lady, ignoring the man as far as you can. Your strategy will depend upon the ability and mobility of the lady. If she is slow, drop-shots and attacking clears should eventually give you or your partner a shuttle to kill. Usually ladies who stand back like this have a good defence and are fairly strong. Therefore you need to get them out of position or off-balance before going for the winner. This can be an interesting tactical situation because a good sides pair do not stick strictly to that formation. Sometimes the lady stays in at the net for several points. At others her partner runs across to take clears, particularly if he is right-handed and is moving from his left to his right. Usually the sides pair will have had a lot of practice at playing against the usual formation and will, therefore, have some advantage, but the back and front pair should win most of the time. It requires a very strong and athletic lady to play a singles against two players even if she has less than half the court to protect.

Returns of service were dealt with at some length in an earlier chapter but it is worth mentioning two points here. It is the man's responsibility to frighten the living daylight out of the lady when she is serving to him—if the match matters. This quite definitely does not mean hitting her with the shuttle, unless the return is a gentle push into her body. Mark you, he must do the same to the man, but it is more difficult to do this because the man feels much less 'exposed' than the lady at the front. An alternative method, which appeals to the Machiavelli in some men, is to bewilder the opponents with subtle and sudden changes of direction and pace. Some have a natural penchant for this. A few develop a wide variety of trick shots which are useful until their opponents learn their repertoire or learn not to commit themselves until the shuttle is played. But these few should not deter the many from acquiring deceptive (but not habitual) returns of service.

Another point to be considered is a high service to the lady.

If she has not got a wide variety of strong overhead shots, her best return is a straight attacking drop into the tramlines, hard enough to get past the lady at the net. Immediately she hits the shuttle she must move in to the net towards a point between the centre of the net and the shuttle. She will find the best position by trial and error. If the man clears the shuttle over her head she must resist the temptation to hit it unless she feels reasonably sure that she can deal with it very effectively. Tactically, of course, the man returning the shuttle will try to tempt her to nibble. This is another delight of mixed doubles. It is most satisfying to play a stroke which is just at the limit of the lady's reach, hoping that she will go for it and either play a poor return or obstruct her partner. Even in the best regulated pairs this may lead to sufficient disharmony to ensure that you win the game. These shots may be played to the side or over the head of the lady. The one over the lady's head when she is at the net is usually played to the lady's backhand near the tramlines. She must be almost directly opposite the person playing the shuttle. The shuttle is lifted sharply just beyond the reach of her backhand to drop on, or just short of, the service line immediately behind her. The maximum height of the shuttle is about nine or ten feet, but will obviously depend on the height of the lady. Good players deal with this by leaping and playing a sharp backhand smash, or by turning to the right as they jump to use a forehand smash.

This is a convenient point to leave mixed doubles because the tactical manœuvring involved in these 'temptations' symbolizes the thought, control, variety and speed of reaction and movement inherent in this game. No lady need be cold playing it. No man should be allowed to play if he is merely going to bang the shuttle back and forth without any thought for his partner.

11

MEN'S AND LADIES' DOUBLES

MEN'S AND LADIES' doubles are basically similar tactically and I will therefore deal with them as one. But there are some differences which must be considered and variations on the basic theme that players should know about.

Elements of Tactics

In mixed doubles, pairs play back and front to take advantage of the ladies' deftness and the men's strength. But this is a weak formation in defence because the man at the back may need to cover the whole width of the court. It is, however, an effective attacking formation because there are few returns from attacking strokes that one or the other of the pair is not in a position to play. If two players of similar strength and ability were playing together, they could defend most effectively if they played side by side, and each defended half the court. They would have very short distances to move to return fast attacking smashes; they would have time to reach drop-shots and time to go back to deal with clears over their head. But as an attacking formation it is weak, because the opponents can so easily play shots to the net which the attackers cannot reach in time to kill.

Now, if we can arrange that a pair adopts an attacking (back and front) formation when they can attack, and a defensive formation (sides) when defending, we can provide the pair with the best chance of winning. But the pair would need to learn to recognize an attacking opportunity or a defensive situation before it arrived so that they could adopt the appropriate formation.

A side may attack as soon as they are able to hit the shuttle down. They then have a chance to force their opponents to play the shuttle from below net level, or to play a weak return which can be hit while it is above net level. It does not matter whether the attacker is playing a smash, drop-shot, drive or attacking clear. If, for instance, you can force a player with a weak backhand to play a backhand return, you should either win the point because he cannot return the shuttle or because you get a weak return that you can kill. Therefore as soon as your opponents are forced to play a defensive or weak shot, you and your partner should be ready immediately to adopt an attacking formation. For example, if your partner goes back to deal with a high clear, you must move in to the net to be ready to attack any shots you can reach—in other words, to play the lady's part in mixed doubles. As long as your side remains on the attack you should remain at the net and your partner at the back. But if your side is in a back and front formation and either you or your partner is forced to play the shuttle upwards, both of you must immediately move into defensive positions (sides). Obviously if you both move to defend the same side of the court you will achieve little and you must therefore develop some system to decide who should move where. The player moving out from the net usually has the most difficulty in dealing with smashes; so he must have priority to decide which side he will move to. It is seldom that the net player is in the centre of the net; he tends to be to one side or the other. Therefore he usually moves back on the side on which he is playing, i.e. he takes the shortest route. His partner takes the other side.

When a side changes over to attack, a similar commonsense arrangement applies. The player in the right-hand court moves in to return net shots, unless the shuttle is well to the left of the centre of the net. Similarly the player on the left moves to take the shots at the back, unless the shuttle is well to the right of the court (see figure 16).

You must get into the habit of changing formations quickly so that you and your partner are in the right place at the right time. In a fast game you can't pause to think about

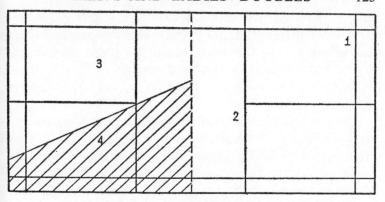

16 Player 3 should cover the unhatched area while his partner, 4, covers the hatched part

where to stand; the movement must be as habitual as the stroke.

Having got into the right position on the court, you need to play the appropriate stroke to take advantage of your position and to maintain, or regain, the initiative. If you are attacking, you should avoid smashing across court, unless the player on that side cannot deal easily with smashes. A smash to any position between the side lines and the centre will limit the returns the opponents can play, provided the smash is strong enough and the player at the net is capable of dealing effectively with returns to the net and also cross-court returns. Any overhead drop-shots played by the attackers must be disguised and accurate so that the opponents cannot attack them. If either attacker is forced to clear, the shuttle must travel both high and deep enough to give the partners time to move into a defensive position. It should also be so deep that their opponents will have difficulty in smashing it.

If you are defending in a sides position, against a back and front attacking pair who have the strokes and mobility to play this formation effectively, you will be limited to playing against straight smashes, a straight return to the net, or a half-court return, or a high return to either back corner of the court. The strokes that are most likely to get you on to the attack are straight shots that will drop close to the net, drives that will get past the player at the net (because of their speed), or shots that will return the shuttle straight to the player at the back of the court before he has recovered from his smash. You must be constantly on the alert for opportunities to play these shots and get on to the attack.

Pairs usually decide beforehand on their 'defending policy'. Who is going to take the shuttle down the middle? Should they think basically of defending backhand or forehand? Who has the best defence and therefore which of them do they want the opponents to smash at when they are forced on to the defensive? In passing, it is worth noting that, with practice, most people find it easier to defend on the backhand. The swing is shorter than on the forehand, and many players find that they can cover a wide range of defensive strokes from those far out on the left to those in front, or even to the right, of the right foot. Defence on the forehand has much less flexibility.

This short description of the game and its tactics will show that the formations of back-and-front attacking and sides defending may be used only if the two players have a wide variety of effective shots, and the speed and anticipation to get them to the right part of the court at the right time. If you are not yet of this category, it is quite possible that these tactics will prove more of a hindrance than a help.

Consider ladies' doubles as an example. Most ladies are not quick enough to cover the whole width of the back of the court really effectively. They find it particularly difficult to move into the backhand corner and play a forehand overhead shot. Most shots into that corner have to be played backhand and many ladies do not have a backhand. They must, therefore, construct their game so as to protect that corner. Ladies are often not strong enough to play effective smashes or really deep clears. A back-and-front formation in these circumstances would be the greatest encouragement you could give to your opponent.

This brief introduction contains the essence of men's and ladies' doubles. Once you have grasped the principle, you will not require much practice to create the backbone of an effective game, provided you have developed the strokes adequately. In the following paragraphs the elements of doubles are examined in much greater detail.

Changing Formations

Most players who are learning the game have some difficulty in deciding where they should be on the court and when they should change formations. Imagine that there is a ring fixed to the floor half-way along the net and that a rope passes through it and joins the two players. The rope is just long enough to enable them to stand in their sides position. If one player goes back to reach a shuttle cleared over his head, the other is immediately drawn in towards the net. If the net player clears from the net and backs out to his defensive position, he will immediately pull the player at the back forward towards a sides formation. The analogy cannot be carried too far but it conveys the essential elements of changing formations. The pair must work together; if one moves, the other must adjust his position. This adjusting must take place immediately, because in-between positions are weak ones and, more important, you can gain the full benefit of the change only if you are in position before the opponents play their return. Thus if you are sides (defending) and force the opponents to clear, the player who has to go in to the net must move immediately he knows that a clear is being played to his partner. Exactly when he will know will depend on the circumstances.

If, for example, the defenders play a cross-court return to a smash and it is obvious that the opponent is going to reach the shuttle at full stretch below net-level, it is also patently obvious that he cannot play an attacking shot. He may play a clear, a drive or a stroke to the net. The sides formation could cope very well with the first two but not the last. Immediately the cross-court drive gets past the player at the net, the person who played the drive must move in to the net very quickly. But if he goes too far across court in the direction of his drive, he will leave an opening for a cross-court drop-shot return. He must, therefore, temper his enthusiasm so that he is not caught. In this case he knew he had to change formation well before the opponent struck the shuttle.

Sometimes in a hard-hitting rally the defence push the shuttle firmly over the net, forcing the net player to return it at full stretch. Some net players decide in this situation to play a clear and flick the shuttle sharply over the defenders' heads. In these circumstances, no notice is given at all, but one of the defenders must react immediately by going back to deal with the clear and the other must move in to cover the net. This is the opposite extreme to the situation described previously, in that no forewarning was given of the defensive stroke.

Another example is the situation in which the defenders again return the shuttle to the net but the net player decides to play a drop-shot. One of the defenders immediately dashes in to deal with it. In all probability he is going to play a clear which means that he will have to return to a defensive position. Why should his partner move to take the 'back' position of a back-and-front pair? Surely they are still defending and should still be in a sides defensive position? This is logical in a way, but not practical. If the player remains in his sides position and his partner decides to play a net return, there are plenty of wide open spaces for the opponents. If the partner plays a poor clear and decides to stay at the net because he will not have time to come out, his partner should be in a position to cover the whole of the court in the hope that he can scramble the shuttle back. Few situations are really hopeless and they are even less hopeless if the players are in the best position. It gives a tremendous lift to a pair if they survive a seemingly impossible situation. It does the opponents' blood pressure no good at all, particularly if the point was important and they had worked hard for it. The scoring aspect is also important. If it was a close match and the opponents had served and won the rally, you would have needed to win two rallies (one to win service and one to win a point) to balance the situation. In a close match each point matters.

You might like to work out why a player must move in towards the net in three cases: when a flick service is played to his partner; when the defending player has played a good drop-shot to the net against a smash which the opposing net player will obviously reach comfortably but the shuttle will be well below net level; when a net shot has been played against a low service.

The need to move immediately into a defensive position is usually fairly obvious. The critical factor often is creating time to get into position before the opponents play the return. It may seem superfluous to suggest that, if a side is in difficulties, the clear that they play should make full use of the height of the hall and the length of the court. Yet how often are players tempted to play a much flatter shot into a corner, in the hope that they will get the shuttle past the player at the back, and how seldom do they succeed. If you pause to think about it, a player must be well out of position if you are going to succeed, unless there is a fundamental weakness in his game.

As I have already mentioned, the player at the net tends to be to one or other side of the centre during play. Thus he usually moves straight back to a sides position. Sometimes, however, he will be in the centre, in which case various factors will influence him in deciding which side to take. For example, if his partner clears from deep in the backhand corner, he will move back towards the forehand side. If he himself has cleared the shuttle from the net to the opponents' forehand corner and knows that his partner is placed centrally behind him, he will usually move out to the forehand side of his court, and his partner merely has to step across to the backhand side to be ready for the smash that will travel the shortest distance.

There will be occasions when the situation is not at all clear-cut; players then must do what they think best at the time and discuss the situation afterwards with their partner. I have heard many acrimonious arguments based on the premise that a situation was sufficiently definable as either attack or defence for one particular action to have been taken. The contestants have appealed to me for a decision and on close examination it has become clear that the situation was really quite indeterminate, so much so that there was no right answer. Not for one minute would I want to stop all arguments about badminton; life would be dull indeed if this occurred. But many arguments are quite futile because neither party can be right.

Many of these arguments would have been avoided, of course, if more clearly definable shots had been played. I have already mentioned a clear. Similar comments could be made about net shots that do not hug the net, and smashes that are either not hard enough or so flat that they might more accurately be described as overhead drives. If the shots are not easily identifiable it is almost certain that the partnership will get into difficulties playing this formation of doubles.

Attack

The player at the back has quite a lot to think about. He must attack weaknesses in his opponents; he must try to force a weak or a short return which he or his partner can kill; he must avoid giving the opponents an opportunity to play flat returns past his partner at the net. All this limits the variety of strokes he may play and also limits their direction. His opponents will be well aware of this and have placed themselves in their sides position ready to deal with the probably attacking strokes. They will probably try to cover their own weaknesses; but they will also try to put pressure on the attackers by closing all the possible gaps into which an attacking stroke may be played. In these circumstances control of pace and direction becomes vital.

Faced with this situation, the attacker sometimes lashes at the shuttle with sickening violence, hoping that some miracle or providence will enable him to produce a brilliant stroke which will demolish his opponents' defence. This succeeds some of the time, of course, and it does provide the player with some healthy exercise. But there are obvious limitations in the method, if the hope is to win games with any consistency. There are difficulties. He knows the opponents have their defence well buttoned up and he has not got time to work out how to unfasten it; therefore he will deal with the situation habitually or instinctively.

It will be useful, therefore, to consider various 'unfastening' processes so that the attacker can do most of his thinking beforehand.

First of all, try to list your assets: how good is your control of speed and direction; have you got pace but no control; are your overhead shots particularly deceptive, and so on. If you have the will and the time, find an opportunity of developing your present assets and creating new ones.

A sides defence presents gaps at the net, at the back of the court, at the sides and down the middle. The gap at the back may be attacked only if the opponents are out of position, or you can catch them with an unexpected flat clear. The gaps down the sides are usually well protected unless the shuttle is directed very close to the side lines. The gap in the middle may be well protected, but there may be some hesitation as each player waits for the other to return the shuttle. The gap at the net may be attacked by the faster drop-shots but the floating drop-shot should be used only if the opponents are particularly slow. There is often a weakness close to the body; the defenders can be forced to play cramped strokes.

The process to use during a game is one of experiment, using your assets to find the means of opening the defence. Probe at the gaps until you find the weaknesses. Speed with little control is only useful if the opponents cannot cope with it. The better the standard of play, the less is this likely to be so. Begin to acquire control by smashing to the right of your opponent then to the left, and then straight at him. Gradually you will find that control develops. The degree of control will depend mainly on your persistence in practising. Try using pace to see whether it causes difficulty. Continue to use it, but try different heights and directions until you find those that give you the best chance of winning the rally. If you continue to experiment like this you will find that when the shuttle comes to you, you know more or less what to do with it.

If your control of pace and direction is good, do make use of it. But do try also to develop a 'big bang', because subtlety alone will not be sufficient armament in the higher classes of the game.

Because control achieves so much at lower standards, players often leave the development of pace until too late and are thereby restricted to a lower level of play than their natural abilities warrant. The use of this asset of control will vary from situation to situation, but one example will show what I have in mind. Play a firm smash as far away from your opponent as possible, in the hope that he will be really stretched and play a short or flat return to you. Aim the next smash at his tummy, hoping that it will reach him before he has recovered from the previous stroke. It may require several strokes to either side of him before he is sufficiently off-balance for the final stroke to be played. Change of pace is another aspect of control used in most sports. It may mean either a sudden increase or decrease in speed. The increase is used when your opponents have got used to your pace and have adjusted their rate of preparation to the speed of your attack. A sudden very hard smash may catch them off-guard and, although it is unlikely to win the point outright, frequently produces a return which may be killed. The slower pace is often introduced into a rally during which the smashes and returns have developed a rhythm. The slower stroke must not be so slow that it is obvious or gives the opponents time to check their stroke and play another one. In fact, it must be almost the same pace as the smash it replaces and should travel along a very similar line so that the defenders will have little indication that there is any difference.

Control is particularly useful when attacking the centre. There often is a point at which the responsibility for strokes to this area shifts from one player to the other. It is worthwhile exploring to see if such an area exists, for the obvious reason that each player may leave the shot to the other. Try varying the height as well as the direction of these strokes.

Drop-shots must be produced deceptively otherwise they will present little difficulty to the opponents. Go for the corners or the centre of the net to make the defenders travel the maximum distance and to cause confusion if possible. A sliced cross-court drop-shot to the centre is occasionally useful in that it often appears to be travelling farther and faster than is the case. Each player may leave it for the other or the player diagonally opposite the attacker may move forward to meet it only to find that he has to travel much farther than he had realized.

Defence

I have already made some comments about defence earlier in this chapter. I will not repeat them here, but go on to examine other aspects of defence.

It is important that the defensive positions you take up on the court are not too far back from the net, otherwise there is little chance of attacking the smash as it will be too near the ground by the time it reaches you. The opponent at the net will have time to see your returns and so will his partner. An advance of even one foot can make a considerable difference. Therefore keep edging forward, giving the attacker less and less space to put his smash into and don't be too worried if an occasional clear catches you out. As in receiving service, you will find that you need to adopt slightly different positions against different opponents.

The defensive formation, as I have explained, is usually described as 'sides', but in fact good pairs are seldom strictly in this position. It should be possible for one player to edge closer to the net than his partner, because the diagonal smash has so much farther to travel. This is a strategy to adopt once you have gained confidence in your ability. It has the consequence, of course, that the player directly opposite the smasher bears the greater responsibility or has more difficulty in covering shots to the back of the court.

Some players develop an instinct which helps them to anticipate the probable direction of the smash. Hence, even in top-quality doubles, you may see the defender diagonally opposite the attacker moving in towards the net to cut off the cross-court smash. In these circumstances one would expect the attacker to play anything but a cross-court smash. In fact he often seems unaware of the defender's movement, and loses the rally.

At some time or other, even the best players are forced to play a weak or short return which does not give them time to move to their best defensive positions before their opponents play the shuttle. This can happen when a low service is attacked and the defenders scramble the shuttle back to about half-court. In theory that should be the end of the rally. But, on the principle that the rally is never lost until the shuttle is 'dead', the defenders will try to organize some form of defence. If the server has followed his service in towards the net, it is usually best for him to stay there and let his partner cope as best he can. If he does try to back out, he will be a sitting target and have the greatest of difficulties in making a stroke at the shuttle. If, however, he has not moved in far, and the shuttle has been returned by his partner into the court diagonally opposite him, he should get out as quickly as possible, keeping his racket ready for a backhand stroke at waist-level or lower; and it is quite astonishing how often the shuttle is played straight at his racket. However, do try to stop moving backwards just as the smash is played. The shuttle is only half-court and the smasher should be able to get it on the ground well in front of the centre of the court, so there is a risk that you may go too far back. But a more serious risk is that you will still be moving backwards while you are trying to play your stroke and will not get any pace into the shot. Any shot that you do play should be directed away from the player at the net.

The need to control the shuttle, even when under pressure, is obvious. There are occasions, of course, when it is quite impossible, but they arise much less often than one would suppose. The easiest shots to return when under pressure are often those that are travelling fairly quickly, because the defender can concentrate all his attention on directing them, for the slightest flick will suffice to get them over the net. It is much more difficult when there is no speed on the shuttle, when the defender is at full stretch, but somehow or other has to coax it back over the net. In some circumstances, therefore, the speed of the shuttle can be of positive advantage to the defender; the attacker can then create a winning situation only if he combines speed with direction, thus forcing the defender to move so far so fast that he is forced off-balance and is unable to recover before the next shot.

Not only must the direction of defensive returns be controlled, but length is also most important. When in difficulty, it is usually much more effective to play a shot to the net than to cock one up half-court, where it can be murdered by an opponent.

But most of the time you will not be defending at full stretch. In easier circumstances, the defenders must think of using the whole court, they must pinpoint the weakness in the attack and try to use that knowledge whenever possible. This requires that the defenders have control of a wide variety of defensive strokes. But how often do we react habitually to a particular situation and clear or drive the shuttle back, regardless of our opponents' abilities? For instance, it is quite common to be faced with opponents of unequal strength and we may want to concentrate our attention on the weaker one. This is often not as easy as it seems and is, of course, governed by the relative strength of all four players on the court. Only if one of the opponents is very weak will you want to give him the attack as a deliberate policy.

We can approach the problem logically by considering particular situations. Often both sides will be back and front, manœuvring for position, and you may be forced to clear. The only time you can be sure that the weaker player will be at the back is when his partner has served a low service and the formation has not changed since then. Having cleared to the weaker player, you must take advantage of his weakness, but he will be seeking opportunities to change places with his partner. These opportunities usually come on the forehand. Against a shortish clear, for instance, he may play a quick straight drop and follow it into the net, calling to his partner as he does so. Similarly against a push shot down the side line he may play a very accurate drop-shot, call to his partner and change places. The tactically intelligent player waits for the opportunity that gives him a reasonable chance of getting to the net without getting the partnership into difficulty. The strategy of the defenders must be to deny him the opportunity by clearing deep and avoiding push returns that he can reach easily. They may also move him across to the backhand side because the change is usually more difficult from that side.

Sometimes a side which has the attack is forced to relinquish it but want to lose as little advantage as possible by clearing to the weaker player. During the game they will have found that the defence facing them is organized with the weaker player on the forehand side. He will tend to go in to the net to return drop-shots, while his partner will move back and across to take the clears. Thus, drop-shots that are well over towards the opponents' backhand side of the court and clears deep into the forehand will tend to pull the stronger player into the net and push the weaker one to the back. The opponents will naturally try to manipulate the attackers so that the shuttle is opposite the stronger player. From here it is very difficult to play a cross-court clear that will not end in disaster, because your partner at the net will not have time to move out into his sides position. Thus you may be forced to clear to the stronger player. In passing, it is worth noting the lesson to be learned. When attacking an uneven partnership take the first opportunity to move the attack across to the side of the court on which the weaker player is. Do it by playing attacking drop-shots to the centre of the net or smashes down the centre from which you hope to get straight returns towards the backhand. This process of attacking the weaker player and starving the stronger often results in the stronger one playing a poor shot when the shuttle eventually comes his way.

Net Play

Net play has been dealt with separately in detail, but there are some points that are of particular relevance to men's and ladies' doubles. When the shuttle is returned to the net from a defensive sides formation, the players usually remain in that formation until they are reasonably sure what the next shot is going to be. The exception is when the shuttle is directed so far away from the net player that he reaches it below net-level and must play an upward stroke. This shuttle must be followed in to the net because the sides pair have, potentially, gained the offensive and they must thus move into a position to attack any shots played upwards from the net. The best formation for this is back and front.

Returns that are rising as they cross the net must be killed swiftly and effectively. But those that are travelling low and almost horizontally as they cross the net create difficulties because many players hesitate, thinking the shuttle will hit the net. Others hold back for fear that their rackets will hit the net if they play a stroke. The result is that the shuttle is allowed to travel about a foot beyond the net before a stroke is played. It cannot now be hit downwards. A drop-shot is a possibility, or a drive at the opponents' face or body, or else a diagonal push into the tramlines. But the pressure has been taken off the defenders when there was a probability that the rally would be ended. It is obvious, of course, that the shuttle should be taken as it crosses the net. If you do not think that you can do this without hitting the net, you will have to practise until you can. In my experience, the problem is confidence rather than ability. Once you have the confidence you will find that you can in fact play quite a range of strokes very easily in this situation.

If the net player is forced to play a net return it is worthwhile trying to draw in to the net the player you want to have there. It may be the opponent who is the weaker net player or the one who tends to play clears from the net rather than indulge in net rallies. You may also take this opportunity of pulling the stronger player in to the net hoping to get a return which can be played to the back of the court to cause the greatest difficulty to the weaker player. Unless this thoughtful approach to net play comes naturally to you, you must try quite deliberately to cultivate it. Be simple and direct in your thinking to begin with; e.g. decide which player is weaker at the net and determine that he will be drawn there if net rallies become inevitable.

You may then find that you win enough points at the net to encourage you to organize the game to give you lots of net rallies against the weaker opponent.

Other Formations

Strict Sides

If neither partner is strong enough to cover the whole of the back of the court and neither has a good smash, strict sides is a possible compromise. Each player takes a side of the court and is responsible for all shuttles on that side; the division is from back to front down the centre line. The tactics the players must adopt are similar to those of singles, particularly if their opponents are also playing sides. They must avoid smashing until the opportunity for an almost certain winner appears, otherwise the opponents may easily return the shuttle to the net. Good clears, deceptive drop-shots, a cast-iron defence and fairly nimble feet are the requirements for the game. The strategy is to get the shuttle well behind, or, near ground-level, well in front of the opponents so that they will play a weak return which you can play into an empty court before they have recovered their balance. The basic service is usually a high one because the low and flick services can be so easily returned to the net and these returns give the server and partner the least possible time to get to the shuttle. The high service allows appreciably more time. While one partner is serving, the other will stand near the centre of the other half of the court. The server usually stands in the middle of the service court to serve. Nothing is gained by going close to the front service line unless the server finds it easiest to serve to a length from there. Immediately the shuttle has been struck, the server must get back to base in the centre of his half of the court.

The only time when the strict sides organization is deliberately altered is in net play. Quite obviously when one player goes in to the net and plays a cross-court net shot, he must follow the shot along the net while his partner, temporarily, looks after the back of the court.

Against an attacking back-and-front pair, the objective of the sides pair is to eliminate the net player from the game—unless there is a positive advantage in bringing him in—and to wear out the player at the back. In one way the sides pair have an advantage in that they will have had much more experience of dealing with the situation than their opponents.

It is interesting to note the 'gaps' in a sides pair to which defensive returns may be played, see figure 17.

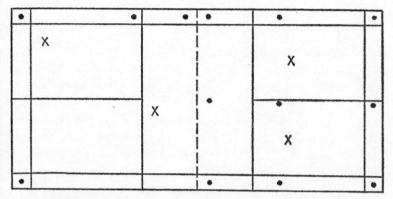

17 The dots in the illustration represent the points to which defensive returns may be played. If the sides pair are attacking, and remain in roughly a sides position, they must leave many gaps in their court. The back and front attack limits the gaps to which defensive shots may be played

I have placed the two sides players in their 'best' position. In practice one (whoever played the smash) would still be towards the back of the court when the return was played and would leave an enormous gap between himself and the net. The back-and-front pair is much tighter, but only if the smash played by the player at the back is strong enough, accurate enough and not played across court.

The game to play against a sides pair is to drop and clear until a good opportunity appears for a smash. Usually the sides pair develops stone-wall defences which are impervious to straightforward smashing. Therefore make them move to the shuttle all the time. Try to pull one in to the net so that your partner may flick the shuttle over his head; or force him to play a weak return from the back of the court. Quite often it is useful to concentrate upon one player, probably the weaker one, and then try to catch the other unawares with unexpected shots. Observe closely which of your shots they tend to anticipate well; then either eliminate them or change the pace, trajectory or direction unexpectedly.

Round-and-Round

In this variation, the motion is usually anti-clockwise. The strictest interpretation of the system requires the players to behave as if they were at the opposite ends of a compass needle. Thus, if one player, A, is at the back returning a shot that is high and deep to his forehand, his partner, B, will be on the front service line, a little to the left of centre. If A plays a straight drop-shot he must follow it into the net. Let us follow him on a possible circuit. He plays a cross-court net shot against the return to his drop and follows that across court to play a clear from the net shot return. Immediately he retreats to a sides position, then moves back to the backhand corner to take the clear played to him. If his smash is cleared high across court he will find himself back in the situation from which he started. His partner would have been moving round to balance him all the time.

As I see little value in this particular formation I do not propose to consider it in any detail. Suffice it to say, it requires the same strokes and positional ability that the standard method requires but demands more movement from the players without any compensating benefits.

Ladies' Doubles

Because they tend to be less powerful and usually do not move as quickly as men, ladies need to adapt, slightly, the tactics I have been describing.

A specific weakness is the backhand corner because ladies usually do not have strong backhands, nor can they move quickly into that corner to play a round-the-head forehand stroke. Ladies adopt various ploys to protect the weak backhand corner. They may make sure that they do not clear the shuttle into their opponents' forehand corner when the opponent is obviously going to reach it early enough to attack the weakness. They avoid services that will expose the weakness. They also place themselves on the court so as to be able to return shots, aimed at the weakness, by getting to them early. All these are limitations on their game which will not be eliminated unless the opponents are too weak to attack the backhand corner, or the ladies improve the speed of their footwork and the effectiveness of their overhead strokes. I can remember clearly a county match in which one lady repeatedly used this weakness to create handsome openings for her partner, having found that her smash could not penetrate the opponents' defence. She manœuvred the game so that she received a clear to her forehand on the forehand side of the court. She might then play a fast flat attacking clear straight along the tramlines. The reply was usually a clear. She then played another straight clear or a drop-shot. The rally seldom lasted more than another stroke or two because the opponent she was attacking was off-balance or out of position, making a kill fairly easy. During the whole of the rally her partner remained at the net to cut off drop-shots. They could afford to do this because they were sure that their opponents could not produce an effective smash against a fast clear into the backhand corner. This illustrates how important drop-shots and clears are in ladies' doubles and how they should be used to create openings or win rallies.

There is another aspect of ladies' doubles that must be mentioned. The back-and-front formation and the need to attack have been emphasized so much that players, particularly young players, do not think of the benefits of defence. Thus one may see four young ladies on a court, all using a low service followed by push shots and drives. The rallies are often very short and the pair with the quicker reactions usually wins. What would happen if one pair went on to the defensive for a few points and served high, or returned shots really high and deep to the corners? In my experience the result is devastating, provided the clears really are deep. Players put into this unaccustomed position at the back of the court find that they do not know what to do with the shuttle.

In ladies' doubles I have frequently seen a good server relax and produce sloppy low services because she feels certain that the opposing lady will not attack her. She is right, of course. The opponent receiving the service will not attack. But the server must take advantage of this situation, not let it slip away. The more accurate the service, the less time the receiver has to reach it and the farther she has to travel. She has to move more quickly to it than to a bad one. If, by varying the direction of the low service, the server can make her opponent hurry her stroke even more, the attacking side is likely to gain an advantage, which may mean that the opponent will try to anticipate the service in future. This will make her susceptible to a flick service and prevent her from anticipating the low one. All this may seem a little far-fetched because there may seem to be so little difference between a shuttle that falls a foot or so inside the service court and one that lands nearly on the line. When coaching in many clubs and on many courses I have experimented with this particular situation, and I have found that I gain an advantage if all the time I try to serve as accurately and as intelligently as I can.

THE COMPLETE PLAYER

SO FAR WE have considered the equipment needed by the player, i.e. racket, etc., strokes, knowledge and use of tactics. This leaves two aspects, physical and mental, that need to be examined.

Physical

I suppose the basic argument here is between those who consider playing the game is the best means of becoming fit and those who claim that additional systematic exercise is necessary. Regardless of the merits of either side they would both agree that a player who wants to play the game well needs to be fit.

In an attempt to avoid becoming involved in the player's emotional attitude towards badminton, I thought it would be useful to look at some other games.

The English football team won the World Cup in 1966. I wonder if they would have done so if their training had merely been playing football? One can never know the true answer to this question, but I think that there would be few in the football world who would have any doubt about the answer. Australia has produced a remarkable crop of tennis players since 1948. Would they have achieved what they did without additional exercise? Again, one will never know the answer, but I suspect that Sedgman, Hoad, Rosewall and Laver would have an opinion. Of course this is only part of the argument. The other is concerned with the type of game that is produced when fitness becomes important. The claim is that the game loses much of its art because players who are superbly fit, but comparatively strokeless, can then dominate the game. If one looks at tennis, particularly post-war Wimbledon, there is evidence of this in the men's singles. A mighty service, a volley and rudimentary ground strokes would describe many players. (Rudimentary is, of course, a comparative term in this case.) But Tilden argues, in his book *Tennis A–Z*, that the fault was in the American coaching system which he sums up as, 'Hit like hell and run to the net'. Among tennis professionals today one can see tennis in full flower. To quote again from Tilden, 'Tennis matches are won or lost by the sum total of physical condition, courage, intelligence, experience and stroke equipment of a player.' If it is thought that too much emphasis on physical fitness is sterilizing a game, the answer surely is not to decry physical fitness but to train the young player who has very good strokes and tactical ability physically so that a complete player is produced who can play a complete game. 'But the game ceases to be a game then and becomes a business and surely this is to its detriment.' is the next comment. One of our coaches recalls joining a club in the late 1930's of which an All-England champion was a committee member. A quiet court was found for the newcomer and he was given a supply of shuttles. A small piece of paper was placed on the ground and the newcomer told to report when he could get nine out of ten services to land on it. In due course he succeeded and reported. The piece of paper was moved and the process repeated. The story is apochryphal. But since there seems to be no objection to practising strokes in a business-like way, why not physical fitness? Again we are at the point that what matters is a sense of proportion. If fitness is allowed to predominate, there is a risk that play will be boring. But, please, the answer must not be to recover the point of balance by reducing the importance of physical fitness, but rather by improving strokes and tactics. In this chapter under 'physical aspect', we therefore must consider the training necessary for strokes, tactics and fitness.

Of course, it is easy to write here 'improve strokes and tactics'; it is quite another matter to achieve this. Inclination is one of the most important factors. Comparatively few players will indulge in systematic practice of strokes and footwork because it can be terribly boring if done unimaginatively. (I can remember clearly my feeling of rebellion at the scales I had to practise when I agreed to learn to play the piano.) Those who have a driving ambition, a driving determination or a driving coach will probably practise and succeed, even if the practice is presented as a hard, relentless slog. The next paragraphs are addressed to those who like at least a little butter, and perhaps some jam, on their bread.

Take advantage of all opportunities for practice that come your way. If the shuttle is to be returned to an opponent between rallies try to play it into his hand. Use your backhand for this if it is weak. During the knocking-up period in club games, agree with your opposite number to practise particular strokes. As you leave the court, take the shuttle to the baseline with you and play an underhand shot to the net, aiming to land the shuttle on the tape. If you get on to the court before the others, hit the shuttle up to the ceiling forehand, or backhand, whichever is your weakness. As you become more expert at doing this, aim at a particular part of the ceiling and see how often you can hit it. At home, get some empty tins into which a shuttle will go easily and organize an indoor game, serving shuttles into the tins. Arrange them in a pattern and give them different values—but make sure that they are about net height. As you become more expert, you can use tins with smaller openings. If there is room off the court, see how often you can bounce the shuttle on your racket, without moving your feet to follow the shuttle if you mis-hit it. As you become more expert at this introduce other limitations, e.g. you must not stretch to reach the shuttle, or you must not lean or turn your body; until you reach the final stage when you are allowed to move your wrist only. Then try using alternate sides of the racket. This will help your net shots. You will, I am sure, think of many other similar schemes.

If you can get a court for an hour or so, you can play games into which limiting factors have been introduced. Let us assume that you want to practise playing to a length, to the net and to the baseline. You could declare the whole of the doubles service court out, except for service at the beginning of each rally. After the service the shuttle will have to be played into the space between the net and the front service line or into the back tramlines. As you become more expert, you can add other limitations. Straight clears and drop-shots might be forbidden or clears from the net penalized. In deciding on these limitations, the players must consider what strokes they really need to practise.

Defence may be the weakness. If you can muster five players put three in one court (two at the back and one at the net) facing two defenders on the other. The defenders serve high all the time, each side counts the points it wins up to 8 or so. The players can then swop round.

Singles players may work out sequences to practise movement and particular strokes. For instance, A might serve high from the right-hand court on to B's forehand; B would then play a straight clear on to A's backhand, A a cross-court drop-shot to B's backhand, B a straight net shot and A a cross-court clear to B's forehand. This is an example of a continuous sequence. To maintain interest, add an element of competition by playing for points, using the usual laws of badminton as far as possible. When B serves, he would, of course, serve high to A's backhand. In this type of sequence you might consider changing over every five points. As your ability develops you can introduce limitations. For example, all clears must land in the back tramlines or, after playing a stroke, a player must touch a chair suitably placed while on his way to the next stroke. These limitations should be used to provide practice for particular strokes or patterns of footwork.

If ladies have difficulty in pouncing on loose shots at the net they could consider the following practice. It may be played straight across the net or diagonally, but more players can get on to the court if the game is played straight. If it is played diagonally, the sequence might be as follows. C and D stand in the usual position for server and receiver in doubles. C serves to D who must return it low over the net hard enough to fall into C's service court. C must return it similarly to D. After the second stroke either player may leap forward to kill the shuttle as it comes towards her. But they must stay behind the front service line until they decide that a shuttle is loose enough to kill. The points is lost if the shuttle is played into the net, out of the court at the back or sides or into the gap between the net and the front service line. As players become more expert at this, each pair could take a turn using the whole length of the net for the rally after the service.

To develop speed and accuracy at the net there is a method that requires three players and a supply of shuttles (old shuttles are quite suitable). Two players are feeders and take turns at feeding the shuttle to the other player. Between times they collect shuttles from the floor. The shuttles are thrown low over the net like net shots. To begin with, they should be placed within reach of the player who is practising. As he loosens up, throw the shuttle farther and farther away from him. When he fails to return one you should change round.

Having illustrated the type of practice you may consider organizing, I will leave you to work out your own schemes. Most of them require a court and one is not always available, hence other methods have to be used which do not have the interest of the 'games' I have described.

Drives may be practised by bouncing the shuttle off a wall, drop-shots by playing a shuttle back and forward over a rope and service by serving to a mark on a wall. The overhead shots may be developed by practising the swing without the shuttle and judging the force being used by the whistle the strings make.

These suggestions use the game, its patterns and its strokes to develop ability. It is questionable whether this is enough. Geoff Dyson, former Chief National Coach to the A.A.A., has said that 'although most sports require strength and endurance, they are poor developers of these basic qualities'. What do we need to develop the ability for badminton? Perhaps the three S's, strength, stamina and speed, sum up the needs. A little thought will focus our minds more accurately. Most strokes demand a strong wrist flick, to make the racket head travel at maximum speed. Players need to move about the court quickly, on balance and under control. Strokes that are to travel the length of the court need strong, powerful arms and shoulders in addition to power in the wrist. Anyone who has returned to badminton after a long lay-off will know how necessary the stomach muscles are. Players who have back injuries realize the extent to which the back muscles are used. From this brief description it is becoming clear that what is needed is a general state of physical fitness plus special fitness for the wrist, arm, shoulder and legs.

There are various ways of tackling general fitness. The one you use will depend on your inclinations and ambitions.

If you are out for friendly, social evenings in which the badminton is of secondary importance, it is unlikely that I can interest you in any training. If you like playing to win and enjoy competition, there is something here for you. There is also something for those of progressively higher ambitions.

Those with limited ambitions and little inclination to take exercise should consider isometrics. These are exercises in which the muscles are placed under severe tension for a few seconds, but the limb is not moved. While telephoning, for instance, grip the phone as tightly as you can for three seconds. Or hook your fingers under the seat of your chair and tense your muscles as if to force yourself down through the seat of the chair. Stretch your legs out, while sitting, and press your feet firmly together. If you think that there is nothing in this, try that last exercise several times a day for a week. It is important that you use all the force you can muster, and you must keep breathing regularly during the exercise. There is a large selection of books available on the subject.

More active people might consider the Canadian systems—5bx for men (eleven minutes a day) and xbx for women (twelve minutes a day). These are graduated exercises providing a gradually increasing dose, until you reach the limit of your patience or physical ability. Their particular attraction in addition to the short time necessary per day, is their simplicity. There is also a challenge in that the graduation is against age and few people can resist proving that they are younger than their years. This is not always sensible, and the book wisely recommends that common sense be combined with the gradual increase in the number of exercises compressed into the eleven or twelve minutes.

Circuit training is a third possibility. This is also attractive because it requires only a short time to complete, presents a challenge and requires maximum effort. Very little skill is required for any of the exercises, which means that all players can use them and benefit. The following extract from a paper prepared by Ray Williams when he was with the Central Council of Physical Recreation gives a brief description of the system.

'. . . A circuit is an arrangement of exercises, some involving the use of apparatus. The performer tackles the exercises systematically and the order in which they are repeated remains the same. Each exercise is repeated a number of times depending on the individual until one lap is completed. This is then repeated twice more in the same way so that three laps are done, thus completing a circuit.

'The introduction of circuit training should take the following form:

'1. TEACHING: At the first session the performer must be taught the exercises as it is most important that they should be performed correctly.

'2. TESTING: During the second session the person(s) taking part, should be tested to produce a training rate. He performs each activity for one minute as quickly as he can and the number of repetitions is noted. After a minute's rest he tackles the next exercise and so on until all the activities have been done. The figures obtained are then divided by two and this will be the training rate for each activity. Should a performer be unable to continue the activity for one minute the number reached before fatigue compels him to stop is noted.

'3. TIMING: The third session sees the tackling of the circuit proper and on this occasion the performer is timed over the complete circuit. This time is then reduced, perhaps by as much as one third, and the result is called the "target time".

'4. TRAINING: At subsequent sessions the performer strives to reduce the time taken as much as possible and so eventually reach his "target time". Having done this he is then re-tested and the whole procedure, except of course for the teaching session, is repeated.

'For training sessions where a large number of people are participating the best method of administration is to fix the dose at each item and to have three circuits graded as to severity. Cards could be used illustrating each activity and the varying dose written in black, green and red figures. The beginner would start on the black figures and when the target time has been reached he would move on to the green circuit and so on.

'Here are two circuits, one using a good deal of apparatus, and the other with a minimum amount. It must be understood, however, that a great deal of apparatus can be improvised. The doses are given for black, green and red circuits but, of course, performers can still be tested individually.

CIRCUIT A

	Black secs.	Green secs.	Red secs.
1. Steps	10	15	20
2. Jump Heaves	5	8	12
3. Trunk Curls	12	18	25
4. Dorsal Lift (10 lb.)	5	8	10
5. Dumb-bell Jumps (10 lb. in each hand)	8	12	18
6. Press-ups	8	15	20
7. Squat Jumps	15	25	35
8. Hand Walk (parallel bars)	Once in each lap		
9. Squat Thrusts	10	18	25
10. Shuttle Run (5 × 10 yds.)	Once in each lap		

CIRCUIT B

	Black secs.	Green secs.	Red secs.
1. Steps (a strong chair will do)	10	15	20
2. Press-ups	8	15	20
3. Hop 25 yds. on alternate legs	1	2	3
4. Trunk Curls	12	18	25
5. Pull-ups (top of a door)	3	5	8
6. Squat Thrusts	10	18	25
7. Dips (dipping between two chairs, feet supported on a third)	5	10	15
8. Stick Body (head supported on a chair)	10	15	25

'It must be emphasised that these above circuits are only intended as a guide and they can, of course, be adapted to individual requirements. In view of the strenuous nature of the work the "circuit" should generally be done at the end of a training session.'

Circuit training is general fitness aimed at increased efficiency in the muscular, respiratory and circulatory systems. It is not a complete training scheme in itself, but is a valuable supplement to other training. This same comment could be applied to isometrics and 5bx and xbx.

What more is required? Some players add specific exercises to deal with particular weakness if they are not catered for adequately by the basic training. Others top up this basic general fitness training by playing lots of badminton games, arguing that once you are generally physically fit, the only way to become really fit for singles (or anything else) is to indulge in that activity. If one plays an adequate amount of singles this will be reasonably satisfactory but it is obvious that 'adequate' will vary from person to person and 'reasonably satisfactory' may not be enough unless we define the purpose of our training.

If we are unlikely to meet players who are fitter or much better players than we are, an appropriate amount of physical exercise and practice to maintain our standard will probably suffice. But if our opponents are likely to be fitter or more expert, some additional efforts are necessary. Frank Sedgman, in his book *Winning Tennis*, says, 'One further saving grace, in addition to my fitness, was speed of movement behind my service. Some observers were talking of me as "the fastest man on a court", and I was finishing with plenty of speed when most of my opponents had slowed to a walk. My speed wasn't particularly natural, nor had I acquired it through long hours of running. I had built it all in the gymnasium.'

The point I am making, of course, is that you need to acquire more resources than your normal game demands if you are going to carry out an extraordinary task. Playing normal games may not top up the basic training enough if your sights are set on the heights. Hence there is the introduction of activities such as touching a strategically placed chair in between strokes in practice sequences, and also the suggestion of additional physical training in a gymnasium.

This extra training needs expert advice which is outside the scope of this book, but it is, perhaps, useful to indicate why such advice is necessary. Badminton requires strength. It demands an ability to accelerate very rapidly. Sometimes only the wrist is involved for a fierce, quick return; sometimes the whole body will be projected across the court. If there is too much concentration on strength, speed may suffer, because the muscles may have been trained to exercise a great force comparatively slowly. But it may also mean that the weight will increase. Thus the player may develop the engine and body of a ten-ton lorry whereas what he wanted was an 'E' type Jaguar. If you want to do gymnasium work and have difficulty in getting advice on exercises, you may well find that your County Badminton Association has contacts that will be able to help you. Of course, the warning I have given applies only if you intend to indulge in extensive physical exercise or you have your sights set on a place near the top.

Mental

Have you ever come away from a hard match which you have just won feeling on top of the world and fit for several more matches of the same kind? Have you ever come away from a similar match having had the hide tanned off you feeling so physically tired that the one thing you want is rest and quiet? As someone once said, 'to feel tired is not to be tired'.

I can remember clearly the first match I ever played in. I was so nervous that I could hardly sit still, yet when I got on to the court and started playing the nervousness suddenly disappeared. No doubt many others have had the same experience.

Has your confidence suddenly fled in the middle of a game and for no apparent reason?

These are just a few examples to illustrate what we all know, that our mental condition effects our physical performance. The difficulty is in controlling our mental condition. I want to look at three aspects only, concentration, determination and confidence.

Concentration

By concentration, I mean the ability to eliminate from one's mind anything that is not relevant to the task in hand. Learning to concentrate at badminton begins when you are learning the basic strokes and tactics of the game. If you are reading about the game or being coached or practising by yourself, try to keep your mind fixed on what you are doing. If you find your mind or your interest wandering you have three choices: force yourself to concentrate; stop the activity for a while; continue but accept the fact that you are not concentrating. If you succeed with the first choice you do not need to read any more of this chapter; if you stop the activity, there is a risk that you will not develop the ability to concentrate, unless you find that the periods for which you can concentrate are getting longer and longer; if you continue the third activity, I think it doubtful that you will ever learn to concentrate.

On many occasions I have been asked, 'How do you know when you are concentrating?' This is one of those extremely simple questions that are so very difficult to answer adequately, in this case because I have found that people have 'different' symptoms. Therefore my general response is to describe my own experience. If I am reading and become so absorbed in the book that I do not hear when people speak to me, I think I am probably concentrating fairly deeply. If I play games (any game) and find that I have ceased to be aware of anything outside the court or pitch I again consider that I am concentrating. But there appears to be two depths. In the shallower one I am aware of the general noise that may be coming from other courts. In the deeper, the court seems to be surrounded by a dense mist which obliterates everything beyond the game in which I am involved. Others have told me that their opponents seem to get smaller and farther away and that the shuttle becomes very, very distinct. Some still see what is happening in the neighbourhood of the court, but feel quite disconnected from things they see there between rallies. Then there are those for whom the whole environment remains the same but the pattern of the game, and the logic of the necessary strategy suddenly becomes very clear. This 'type' may also find that his physical and mental reflexes have sharpened considerably. But there are things that they all have in common. The opponents become very distinct, their strokes and strategy are easier to read and the shuttle becomes much more visible than usual; errors are reduced and strokes become more accurate; the results of the games are better than usual. All kinds of questions arise from this. How can one concentrate at will? Can it be developed? For how long can concentration be maintained? Should one try to concentrate all the time or reserve the effort for occasions when it really matters?

Let's deal with these questions in order. There is little doubt that some people have the ability to concentrate at will. I do not know whether this ability can be developed although I have no doubt that by making the effort to concentrate players can improve their ability to do so. There is no doubt that concentration can be maintained or the length of a normal badminton match lasting at most three games without a break.

I do not know the answer to the last question about reserving the effort, but it does seem that the answer may vary from person to person. Ben Hogan writing about golf has this to say, 'When you practise go out on the tee with a purpose in mind, not just for exercise. You'll get the exercise anyhow and with a definite purpose in mind you will be adopting habits of concentration which will pay off when you actually play a round. . . . While I am practising I am also trying to develop my powers of concentration. I never just walk up and hit the ball. I decide in advance how I want to hit it and where I want it to go. . . . Try to shut out everything around you. . . . If something disturbs my concentration while I am lining up a shot I start all over again. An ability to concentrate for long periods of time while exposed to all sorts of distractions is invaluable in golf. Adopt the habit of concentrating to the exclusion of everything else while you are on the practice tee and you will find that you are automatically following the same routine while playing a round in competition.' There can be no doubt about Hogan's answer to the question, and anyone who has seen him play will have little doubt about his power of concentration. I could quote many other views giving varying opinions which would confirm the view expressed at the beginning of this paragraph. But one interesting point emerges from all of them. If you want to get to the top, learn to concentrate all the time that you are practising or playing the game. If you have not got the ability to get to the top, concentration will get you further than perhaps you thought possible.

One last thought on concentration. It is difficult to concentrate on something that is boring and practice can be boring unless interest is built into it. We coaches know this only too well, but too often we forget it in our coaching sessions.

Determination

In badminton there have been many games in which players possessing apparently superior equipment all round have been beaten by the 'terrier' who refused to give in. There are some lucky players who are of a determined nature and this becomes evident in much that they do. However, I do not think that I will be challenged if I suggest that they are in the minority. This does not mean that many others do not show determination or that they cannot be determined if the situation demands it. Perhaps this is the key to the situation, 'when they think the situation demands it'. Thus in a tournament, against better players, some have achieved scores that were a surprise to their friends and to themselves. As one young player put it, 'I know I'm going to be beaten but I'm determined to make him work for his win.' He did and played very good badminton in the process. Confidence comes into this situation as well, because the weaker player has nothing to lose. Another factor is involved. The player was in a determined frame of mind before he went on to the court. I am sure that this counts a great deal because just as it is difficult to regain control of a game if you let slip a winning position, it is difficult to call upon your determination when you have slipped into a losing one. This suggests that one should get into the habit of being determined to win or to achieve a particular objective, whenever one goes on to the court. This is probably too much to ask from the casual player, but I am sure it is essential for anyone working their way up the ladder or for someone who wants to stay at the top.

In my experience, determination brings in its train advantages akin to concentration in that it generates a positive outlook. Instead of waiting for openings and winning situations to arise, players search and strive for them and somehow find openings that they did not realize existed before. In my own case, I find that my mind seems to change into a much higher gear. I have also found other benefits; for example, I can make myself reach shots that at other times I would leave and I can develop a 'killer-instinct' which helps to prevent me letting opponents off the hook. To my mind there is no doubt that these examples are assets, hence determination is an asset. Can it be developed? I am sure it can. Just by thinking in a determined way before and during a match makes a difference. Setting reasonable objectives also helps. You may decide, during a club game, to try to dominate an opponent's service or to reach a particular score first. Having set yourself these private objectives try to assess as cold-bloodedly as you can, whether you did in fact reach them. This is much easier to do in a factual situation such as reaching a particular score first, than in situations that cannot be measured. If you achieve what you set out to do, set a stiffer test next time. If you fail, try to accept no excuse within your mind for your failure, regardless of what you may say to others; immediately you start making excuses you weaken your determination and confound the whole object of the exercise. This review I am suggesting does not necessarily consist of a detailed post mortem but of a quick appraisal. If, for instance, you intended to dominate the service, but did not quite achieve this, try to think why this happened. Was the service better and more consistent than you had expected? Were you unable to think of or play returns that would get the opponents into difficulty? Having decided what went wrong, try to think what you are going to do about it. Part of the time the answer will be that you do not know, in which case you might discuss the problem with a more experienced player or with a coach or write to the *Badminton Gazette*. Before you consult any of these, be as clear as you can in your own mind about the problem. It is too vague to say that you were playing men's doubles against X and Y and could not find a means of attacking X's low service. If you state the problem more definitely the answer may sometimes become obvious, but even if it does not you are much more likely to get a helpful answer. The way to form the question is to think where your opponents were on court and how they were standing; where you were and how you moved to the shuttle; how the shuttle was moving towards you—trajectory, speed, direction; what you tried to do with it and with what results. This seems a lot to require in a question, but the positional information is easily conveyed by a diagram on which could be marked the direction of the shuttle and the point of impact. This leaves very little to be conveyed verbally or in writing. You may also want to add your own thoughts on the subject, such as other returns you have considered and rejected. This is all part of the determination to improve, whatever your standard may be. Do try to be honest with yourself, otherwise you will be tending to waste your time either because you fail to recognize faults or because you are correcting the wrong faults. However careful you are, there is always a risk of the latter because few people are able to take an objective view of life; this is a part of human nature and we must put up with it. Determination is often infectious if it can be communicated to the less confident or less determined member of a doubles pair. I well remember discussing prospects with a mixed doubles pair before a vital match. The man was obsessed by the quality of the opposition until his partner lost her temper and said, 'I'm damned if I'm going to be beaten by a reputation before the game starts.' Her determination carried them through three long games to win the third after setting.

When I have discussed the mental aspect of badminton with players, a common conclusion has been reached that concentration, determination and confidence are inter-connected and that it is much easier to concentrate and be determined if confidence is strong. We must, therefore, look at this last aspect.

Confidence

Confidence is a quality with so many aspects that I never feel sure, when discussing it, that any two people are talking about the same thing. This means that it is a subject difficult to write about; it also means that I must try to define my subject in badminton terms. I always think of confidence as an inner certainty about some aspect of the game. Ideally a player should be sure that he is fit to last the game he is about to play; that he has adequate strokes for the task and that he has sufficient control over them to enable him to adopt suitable tactics; that he has tactical ability to use his assets. If he has doubts about the adequacy of any part of his equipment this is liable to affect his confidence. Since these statements are basically comparative because they must be related to a task, it means that a player's confidence will vary with his assessment of the task. Thus different players will find different tasks a challenge to their confidence. It will be useful to look at the commonest situations, subject to the following general comment.

General

If a player can concentrate well and has plenty of determination, he usually has confidence as well. He is confident that he will do as well as he can, even if he does not succeed in winning. As a result, his general standard of play is fairly consistent even if some of his strokes let him down now and again. If a person is the exact opposite, he can have little hope that his confidence will withstand pressure. Most of us will be somewhere in between and should be working to develop our concentration and determination.

Tenseness and Nervousness

In the first case, lack of confidence is usually a secondary effect arising from tenseness or nervousness. It may not arise before the match but may appear if the better player does not settle quickly. If he finds that his nervousness persists on the court it may, for example, prevent his strokes from flowing as they usually would. The more tentative they become, the more mistakes he makes, with obvious consequences. Quite often the situation is not as extreme as those last few sentences would suggest, but the result is similar. There are many suggested remedies, none of which qualify for universal application. But before examining the remedies we must look closer at the difficulty. For some reason his nervousness has made the player think in detail about the quality of his strokes, or his anticipation or his tactical ability or whatever, with the result that he is trying to control the quality of his performance and play a match at the same time. For most people this is not possible, even if they are not involved in a match. It seems that if we rely on the mechanical, habitual co-ordination between eye, brain and muscles, most of our strokes will be produced normally; but immediately we interfere with the process our mechanical ability decreases. The player needs to stop thinking about the particular aspect of his game that is letting him down and let his habitual ability take charge. If strokes have become tentative the player must avoid delicate ones, must avoid trying to play too accurately and should not go for all-out winners, e.g. when smashing. The only parts of the stroke he need think about are the preparation and follow-through. As he moves' to the shuttle, he should be generally aware that he is preparing as he goes and he should allow full freedom to his follow-through. This will help the player to relax his physical movements and when this is achieved he can begin to play with more accuracy and introduce a wider variety of strokes. He will also help himself enormously if he can become absorbed in the game, so that his conscious mind is fully occupied by observation, analysis and strategy. Until he has relaxed he must avoid saying to himself while playing a stroke, 'This must be a good shot or I will be in difficulty!' Unless he does, there is a good chance that the stroke will not be good and his confidence will suffer further. In passing, may I make it clear that the thought I have quoted might be a useful challenge to the determined player full of confidence. At this point I am dealing only with the player whose confidence has been shaken.

Confidence in one's tactical ability and anticipation is rather more difficult because there is no mechanical means of putting it right. The ideal answer is to give yourself more time to think, but normally the situation is that the more you try to do this, the less time there seems to be. The basic difficulty again seems to be some form of interference with the normal mechanisms on which we usually rely. The answer is to restore confidence in the mechanisms so that our mind does not need to interfere. The best advice on the tactical side is to simplify matters as much as possible. Identify the main gaps in your opponent's court and play the simplest stroke available into one of them, preferably the one that will make him play the shuttle upwards. Try not to win points quickly, but keep the shuttle going until an opening appears. Once the opening appears you may go for it. In this way you will often find that you become so involved

in keeping the shuttle going that you relax and your normal
mechanism takes over.

The basic cure for lack of confidence in anticipation seems to
be to avoid talking to yourself in terms of 'What is he going to
do with the shuttle?' and concentrate upon readiness to move
to where the shuttle is likely to be played. I well remember
coaching one lady who was a good server, but always advertised
her flick service by a slight preliminary movement. I played
against her a short time afterwards and was pleased, though
disconcerted, to find that she had eliminated the movement
without impairing her service. There was I, trying to forecast
her flick service without having any recognizable symptoms!
Against others I would have relied on my speed of reaction
until I found I could read the service, and would not have been
bothered about my inability to read it at that stage. But it must
have taken about six services to persuade me to do this against
the lady I had been coaching. It would probably have been
many more had I not remembered the advice to think about
the gaps into which she might serve and to get ready to move
to one of these gaps immediately I knew the shuttle was being
played to it. Usually in these situations the player is trying to
achieve an almost impossible feat, i.e. to anticipate a stroke
without having any indications on which to work. This is so
clearly impossible that I never cease to be amazed that I was
caught in the trap.

Basic Weakness in Your Game

If you know you have a weakness that may be exploited I would
assume that it only causes concern if you know the opposition
can and will exploit it. It may also cause you concern if you are
uncertain about this because you do not know the opponents.
(The long-term answer must be to eliminate the weakness, but
this is not always practicable.)

Stroke Weakness

I once coached at one club where the man in mixed doubles

stood in the backhand corner of the court almost on the base-line, while his partner served. This was to 'protect his backhand'. I may add that it needed protection. Lack of confidence is usually one of several possible consequences of thinking pessi-mistically about one's weaknesses. It makes all the difference in the world if you can find or develop some compensating assets, or if you can devise effective strategies that protect the weak-ness. I have mentioned elsewhere in the book the lady with a poor backhand but nimble feet and excellent round-the-head strokes. Having started to think positively about the situation, analyse it as calmly as possible and then determine to show your opponent at the first opportunity, that you have found an adequate method of protection.

Tactical Weakness

Some ladies at mixed doubles find themselves off-balance if they have to move quickly to a shuttle played to the corner of the net. They are then at the mercy of the opponents unless they can re-cover very quickly. In the extreme case they will be moved back and forward along the length of the net by the man playing ac-curate drops to each corner, until he applies the *coup de grâce*. I am convinced (and have proved this to my satisfaction in coaching) that the main fault is positional, the lady stays cen-trally at the net. The second fault is the lack of readiness to move, and the third is a habit of playing fairly deep cross-court returns against shots to the corner of the net. These invariably go straight to the man who is waiting in the middle of the court and encourage him to begin the sequence of strokes to alternate corners of the net. If comments such as these are made immediately before a game, they will, in my experience, have little effect on most players. They are the basis of the long-term solution. The short-term one is to tell the player to avoid playing to the centre of the court unless there is a big gap; to play strokes down the side lines deeper or shorter than usual and also to encourage the lady to take a chance that a shuttle played straight down the side line will be returned straight to

the net. Her partner must be prepared to go for the cross-court
if the guess is wrong. These are simple positive measures involving both players, and measures that they can encourage
each other, by a word or two between rallies, to continue. The
most important one is to avoid playing to the centre.

If the lady could have analysed the rally in the way that I,
an observer, had been able to, she might well have come up
with the same solution as I did. The essence of the solution
would clearly be contained in a factual account of the sequence
of strokes played. Similarly a simple, straightforward description of other situations can indicate either that players are
creating difficulties for themselves or that a simple alteration in
their game can lead to immediate improvement. If you have
friends who are willing to observe and comment, get them to do
so. But don't ask for their advice on what you should do, ask
for a factual description of what happened.

This approach will not help if your problem is lack of ability.
It will merely indicate what you need to practise.

Stronger Opponent

There is also, similarly, little short-term comfort that one can
offer to a player who is faced with an opponent who has proved
his superiority on many occasions. Concentration, determination and confidence may all be affected. The only effective answer
is the long-term one of improving the standard of the play. In
the short term, the tactical solution depends on the previous
scores. If they have been fairly decisive wins, desperate measures
may be indicated. The weaker player must decide to take a calculated risk, and having decided to do so, stay determined to
carry it through. The particular form of risk will depend upon
his strokes, ability and so on. In singles, he might try forcing
the pace by playing fast flat clears to the corners mixed up with
fast drop-shots. In the same vein he might try quick low services.
If possible he should try to anticipate returns, particularly those
to the net, and again force the pace by his returns. If the scores
have been close there is no real reason for being despondent.

Probably the key is determination and he could usefully start the game with his mind concentrating on the probably pattern of the game, determined to take advantage of any parts of the pattern that indicate openings to him. He must try to dismiss from his mind his own weaknesses except for determining to scramble through such situations as best he can. In my experience it requires only a slight change of fortune or of attitude to tip the balance. You have nothing to lose, and everything to gain.

Summary

It is obvious that concentration, determination and confidence go hand-in-hand. Develop any two and there is a good chance that the third will be added as a bonus. They are assets which can be acquired without hard physical work; mental effort is usually what is required. Every time you go on to the court, you have a chance to improve them. The opportunity exists whenever you think about badminton—should the chance and the opportunity go begging?

Appendix I

BADMINTON IN SCHOOLS

BADMINTON WILL ALWAYS present difficulties as a subject to be taught as part of physical education. A court occupies a large space, but can accommodate at most only four players for a game and a game will last about ten minutes. The equipment is not particularly expensive until the numbers of rackets required for a class are counted and the maintenance costs added on. Shuttles are no particular problem now that plastic and nylon ones are available as alternatives to 'feathers'. I was discussing these problems recently with a retired headmaster who recalled many instances in which similar arguments prevented the introduction of new equipment and teaching methods for quite a long time, until some sudden change of attitude made them generally acceptable. He felt that the whole process bore some similarity to the hostility to changes in ladies' fashion.

In the 1950's it was commonly claimed that badminton was quite unsuitable for schools; yet now in the 1960's, there is agreement between the Badminton Association and the education authorities about the dimensions of gymnasiums to accommodate badminton courts; there are many schools in which the game is played; there are inter-school matches; there is an English Schools' Badminton Association. This is remarkable progress, one for which many teachers and officials deserve our thanks.

If the ex-headmaster's assessment is accurate, there has been a change of attitude towards badminton. I think it has been helped by the recognition that, during school periods, pupils need only be given an introduction to badminton; they need not be taught to play the game completely. If there is sufficient interest in the school, additional instruction may be given during the lunch-break or after school hours. In this chapter, therefore, we need to consider how to provide an introduction to the game during school hours and how to organize play at other times, though each school will, of course, decide what it can do.

The essentials of badminton are a useful starting point to establish what needs to be taught. A player should be generally physically fit and be capable of moving to the shuttle so that he can play a stroke with a free swing. These factors are common to most ball games and if, in general, a pupil can do it for one, he can do it for others. Physical education should cope with his fitness. In addition a player should have a strong wrist for forehand and backhand strokes. As indicated earlier in this book, boys usually have good wrists for forehands while girls tend to be much weaker. Both boys and girls need to develop the strength and facility of their backhand actions. They need to be able to time the shuttle and also direct it. Directing the shuttle involves controlling height, length, direction and speed. Pupils need to be able to hit it hard enough to drive or clear it the length of the court. To play games they also need to have some knowledge of rules and tactics.

The basic skills of hitting, timing and directing the shuttle may be taught in many different ways and each teacher will develop his own method. But it may be helpful if I describe a system based on one used by one teacher who is a National Coach.

To begin with, the class is divided into groups of three. In each group one pupil will feed by hand, one will practise strokes and the third will keep the feeder supplied with shuttles. No court is necessary and the whole length of the gymnasium may be used. To begin with, the stroke should be a wrist movement (not a full swing) at between waist- and shoulder-level on the forehand side. As the pupils gain confidence and efficiency, the swing may be lengthened. Then the same stroke may be practised on the backhand. As soon as possible the grouping should change from three to two, each pupil now having a racket. They may then practise playing the shuttle back and forth across the gymnasium, first forehand, then backhand, and finally using the stroke appropriate to the shuttle they are receiving. In the early stages of this, when the shuttle is not being hit hard, a little overcrowding adds to the general atmosphere of bustle and enjoyment.

Having obtained some form of control of shots between shoulder and knee, the pupils should now try those above shoulder-level. The teacher will know best whether to go back to groups of three and hand feeding, or to continue working in pairs. In my experience reverting to groups of three loses some of the momentum, interest and enthusiasm generated by working in pairs. The individual teacher will also know at what stage pupils are ready to start practising the overhead. It may be helpful to mention that the action above shoulder-level is a throwing one very similar to the one they have been practising. Some pupils will find the transfer very easy, others will find it much more difficult. On the backhand it is easy to start at the first stage again, i.e. using the wrist only, but in my opinion this is not satisfactory on the forehand. On that side one needs to start with the arm and wrist movement together. This is fairly easy if the pupil waits with his racket down his back as in figure 5 (b) and the shuttle is hand fed to an appropriate height. 'Appropriate', in this case, means that the shuttle must be thrown up to a height of three or four feet above the point of impact so that it will drop almost vertically to that point.

When the overhead strokes are being played it is essential that pupils progress to the stage of using their shoulders. They should reach up to play the shuttle and move forward to it.

In introducing these practices, many coaches stress that pupils should be encouraged to develop their natural stroke and not have impressed on them a stereotyped pattern. But it is essential to increase the effectiveness of their natural ability by the encouragement of good habits. This may seem a contradiction and therefore demands a bit of explanation. In preparing for an overhead stroke it does not matter whether the arm is swung under and back as in the traditional tennis service, or whether the racket is placed in the position of figure 5 (b) by a quick horizontal movement. What matters is that the shoulders are turned and the elbow and wrist are cocked in preparation for a full stroke. Another example is a forehand drive. Theoretically it is desirable that the right-handed player steps into the stroke with his left foot leading. During a quick rally there is often no time to do this and the stroke must be played off the right foot. Since body weight is not needed for the stroke, there is no disadvantage in stepping across with the right; using the right foot also gives a positive advantage because of the extra reach obtained.

Some players naturally play their overhead strokes with their feet almost square but in all other respects play an orthodox stroke. Others habitually position themselves so that the point of impact of their smashes is a little to the left or to the right of the normal position. Some have a slow back swing followed by very rapid acceleration of the racket head; some have a fast backswing.

If the variations do not appear to interfere with the efficiency or development of the stroke, I would hesitate to persuade the player to adopt a standard approach.

The method of introducing the practices is important. Even at twelve and thirteen, pupils are aware that 'backhand strokes are difficult'. In talking about the strokes that the players have to practise it is useful to refer to them as being on the right- or left-hand side of the body. Encourage the players to change their grips when playing strokes on alternate sides and you will find that it soon becomes second nature. A good method of practising is to make the pupils twirl the handle in their fingers and stop the movement by taking a forehand or backhand grip.

It will become clear during the practice which pupils are natural players and require encouragement rather than instruction, and which ones require patient application by the teacher. Some of the latter group may make progress if a shuttle is hung from a beam so that they may practise judging distance and thus gain confidence.

Competition should be introduced as soon as possible. If

courts are marked out in the gymnasium, ropes may be hung along their length at net height, dividing them in half. Up to three singles may be put on each court (depending on the size of the pupils) to play games up to seven points, using the laws of badminton as far as possible. Most of the strokes may be used in these games. Competitions to see who can hit the shuttle farthest or who can play it most accurately can also be arranged using strokes that have been taught during the lesson. These competitions may be between individuals or between teams. For instance, the drive may be practised by a class of thirty divided into five groups of six, each group having five shuttles. The teams are lined up on one side of the gymnasium; one member is appointed feeder. Each player hits one drive over a net aiming to land the shuttle between two parallel lines that have been marked on the floor about twenty feet away. After each set of five drives the team counts its score. A new feeder is appointed and the 'game' repeated. Relay races in which the shuttle is played backward and forward along two lines of players facing each other, or in which pupils have to run the length of the gymnasium keeping the shuttle off the ground by hitting it ahead of them are other examples of competitive practices. All have the purpose of developing the ability to play strokes, speed of reaction and control of the shuttle.

Ultimately, of course, the pupils want to have a 'real' game. Usually classes are too large for this urge to be satisfied during class time, and the games have to be organized during lunch time or immediately after school. If there is to be a good supply of potential club players, this step of arranging games is essential because most clubs are not able to accommodate beginners.

If the gymnasium or school hall is not suitable or not available, it is sometimes possible to come to some arrangement with a local club to use their hall and nets immediately after school for a reasonable fee. It is certainly useful to gain the interest of local clubs because their members may be willing to pass on rackets for use by the pupils and some may find time to help with the coaching. These 'helpers' may be an embarrassment if they are enthusiastic but incompetent. The teachers must therefore leave a loophole in any arrangements they make or try to find means of vetting any offers they get.

Clearly the opportunity to play cannot be open to the whole school and may need to be restricted to the upper classes. What a particular school does, will depend on its type and the facilities available.

Part of the time devoted to play should be used for coaching in tactics, particularly when the game is being introduced to a school or a new group are taking up the game at the beginning of the school year. It is very useful, when the teachers are inexperienced players, if local coaches or players can be encouraged to help or play with the pupils. People learn by watching and by doing and the better the example the more quickly are they likely to learn the game. But at some stage, time will be needed for further coaching in the strokes. This is usually difficult because the pupils want to play, not practise, and the practice needs to be almost as interesting as play or seen to be really necessary before they will work at it. One method of demonstrating the necessity is to pin-point their weakness when playing against them and then show how practice will help to strengthen their play. In this process it is important not to destroy their confidence and also not to create a defensive barrier.

Sometimes it is possible to work to a timetable of alternately practising and playing. For example you might begin each session with about five minutes' practice of the backhand (since this is the weakest stroke usually) and then have some games followed by the practice of particular tactics, followed by more games. If there were two or more teachers, one could look after the play while the other coaches those who are sitting out, in footwork or strokes. Although this is very demanding on the energy and time of the teacher, it means that a lot may be packed into a short space.

There are some weaknesses to which young players are particularly prone. Often, when playing doubles, they work as individuals and not as a pair. This is quite natural and most will grow out of the habit. It is, therefore, a matter of discretion whether the teacher deliberately tries to change their outlook.

A positive side of this is that they will usually be very willing to play singles and this should be encouraged wherever possible. Another weakness is losing points through over-ambitious strokes or by trying to play too accurately. In correcting this there is a risk that some players may become negative in their approach and strive to keep the game going until their opponents make a mistake. This approach will pay off until a certain standard is reached, when this type of player will find it impossible to make further progress without a radical change in his game. I would suggest that it is better to train the players to recognize when they have tried for an impossible winner and then help them by discussion and practice to devise alternative methods of dealing with the situation. In my experience the problem is usually that a particular situation demands a particular response from that particular player.

In general, boys have a natural inclination to play hard and aggressively and have an adequately developed killer-instinct. The girls are often quite the opposite. It is sometimes possible to introduce a sense of urgency to girls' games by limiting them to short games—perhaps the first to reach five points wins. It also helps if a speed of shuttle appropriate to their strength is used. Probably the working spirit created by the teacher is as important as anything else.

Exhibitions[1] by good local or county players can be a great help to the teachers. They sometimes fail; the commonest faults are poor organization, lack of purpose and poor play by the participants. The last is beyond the control of the organizer but the first two should cause no difficulty if some time and thought is given to planning the exhibition. Is the purpose to create interest in badminton, to provide an introduction to tactics, to help develop tactical ability or to set standards of play that pupils might try to attain? Once the purpose is clear, the form of the exhibition becomes obvious or, perhaps more ex-

[1] The Badminton Association of England organizes a very good show called 'Focus on Badminton' in areas where there is a demand. Those who take part are near or full internationals. The programme covers demonstration of strokes, exhibition matches and some coaching.

actly, the types of game that are appropriate become obvious. A programme can then be prepared and arrangements made for seating for the spectators. It is important that the organizers make some assessment of the time that will be needed for the games listed in the programme; it is better to overestimate than underestimate the probable length of games. The audience need to know beforehand what is in store for them and will often find a short commentary between games helpful. The commentary can be purposeful if the exhibition has been prepared for that particular audience. A series of disjointed, hurriedly prepared remarks are more of an irritation than a help to the audience; the comments also need to be thought out beforehand. Indeed, several versions may be required to meet various probable happenings during the exhibition.

Sometimes the players are so keen to give a good exhibition that they make many more mistakes than usual and few rallies develop. If they agree between themselves not to attack service too severely until they have settled into their game and also not to go all out for winning shots, rallies develop easily. But there will always be occasions when everything goes wrong in the game; one can but put up with this with as much equanimity as possible.

The types of games need some thought. A hard-hitting men's doubles will usually generate interest and excitement, particularly if there is some small prize to be won. A skilful singles will give satisfaction to those with a good knowledge of the game, but, after a while it is likely to begin to pall with those who do not know the game well. Ladies' doubles sometimes lack the bite of men's and may develop into a tactical battle, which again may fail to interest those who lack experience. Thus the game should, ideally, be adjusted to the needs of the particular audience.

If the purpose of the exhibition is instructional, one might think of the following programme. A short demonstration of the basic strokes with a commentary. Start with the overhead strokes, then the drives, the underhand defensive ones, the net shots, service and returns of service. Keep it short and simple.

Then play an exhibition doubles with no interruption. Follow this by relating the strokes to the game and illustrate how they should be used for attack and defence. Play another game, but this time draw attention at intervals to the use that is being made of strokes, to their direction, pace, trajectory and to the way the players move into position to play the strokes. The next step is to describe the tactics of the doubles game and then to demonstrate them in play. The content of the comments and the form of the demonstrations will depend on the knowledge and experience of the spectators.

Should the pupils watching the demonstration be of a sufficient standard, it is highly desirable that they should have an opportunity of playing with the visitors.

Children often learn games very quickly. They have a tremendous well of energy and enthusiasm. It is heartening to see that in more and more schools these natural assets are being directed to badminton. I hope even more teachers will be tempted to introduce it into their schools.

THE LAWS OF BADMINTON[1]

as revised in the year 1939 and adopted by
THE INTERNATIONAL BADMINTON
FEDERATION
Subsequently revised up-to-date

Court

1. (*a*) The Court shall be laid out as in the following diagram
'A' (except in the case provided for in paragraph (*b*) of this Law)
and to the measurements there shown, and shall be defined by
white, black or other easily distinguishable lines, $1\frac{1}{2}$ in. wide.

In marking the court, the width ($1\frac{1}{2}$ in.) of the centre lines
shall be equally divided between the right and left service courts;
the width ($1\frac{1}{2}$ in. each) of the short service line and the long
service line shall fall within the 13-feet measurement given as the
length of the service court; and the width ($1\frac{1}{2}$ in. each) of all
other boundary lines shall fall within the measurements given.

(*b*) Where space does not permit of the marking out of a
court for doubles, a court may be marked out for singles only
as shown in diagram 'B'. The back boundary lines become also
the long service lines, and the posts, or the strips of material
representing them as referred to in Law 2, shall be placed on
the side lines.

Posts

2. The posts shall be 5 ft. 1 in. in height from the floor. They
shall be sufficiently firm to keep the net strained as provided in

[1] Published by permission of the International Badminton Federation.

DIAGRAM (A)

|1' 6"| --------------- 17'0" --------------- |1' 6"|

Back Boundary Line;

also Long Service Line for Singles

Long Service Line for Doubles

Right Service Court

Centre Line

Left Service Court

Short Service Line

Side Line for Singles

Side Line for Singles

Side Line for Doubles

NET

POST

POST

Side Line for Doubles

Short Service Line

Left Service Court

Centre Line

Right Service Court

Long Service Line for Doubles

Back Boundary Line;

also Long Service Line for Singles

|-------------- 20'0" --------------|

2'6"
13'0"
6'6"
6'6"
13'0"
2'6"

44' 0"

Diagonal Measurement of full Court: 48ft. 4in.
Diagonal Measurement of half Court: 29ft. 8¼in.
(from post to back boundary line)

DIAGRAM (B) Singles Court

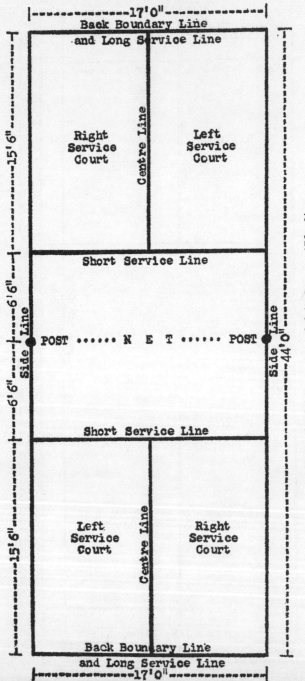

Law 3, and shall be placed on the side boundary lines of the court. Where this is not practicable, some method must be employed for indicating the position of the side boundary line where it passes under the net, e.g. by the use of a thin post or strip of material, not less than $1\frac{1}{2}$ in. in width, fixed to the side boundary line and rising vertically to the net cord. Where this is in use on a court marked for doubles it shall be placed on the boundary line of the doubles court irrespective of whether singles or doubles are being played.

Net

3. The net shall be made of fine tanned cord of from $\frac{5}{8}$ in. to $\frac{3}{4}$ in. mesh. It shall be firmly stretched from post to post, and shall be 2 ft. 6 in. in depth. The top of the net shall be 5 ft. in height from the floor at the centre, and 5 ft. 1 in. at the posts, and shall be edged with a 3-inch white tape doubled and supported by a cord or cable run through the tape and strained over and flush with the top of the posts.

Shuttle

4. A shuttle shall weigh from 73 to 85 grains, and shall have from 14 to 16 feathers fixed in a cork, 1 in. to $1\frac{1}{8}$ in. in diameter. The feathers shall be from $2\frac{1}{2}$ to $2\frac{3}{4}$ in. in length from the tip to the top of the cork base. They shall have from $2\frac{1}{8}$ to $2\frac{1}{2}$ in. spread at the top and shall be firmly fastened with thread or other suitable material.

Subject to there being no substantial variation in the general design, pace, weight and flight of the shuttle, modifications in the above specifications may be made, subject to the approval of the National Organization concerned.

    (a) in places where atmospheric conditions, due either to altitude or climate, make the standard shuttle unsuitable; or

    (b) if special circumstances exist which make it otherwise expedient in the interests of the game.

(*The Badminton Association of England has approved the use of modified shuttles (e.g. plastic, nylon, etc.), for play in England.)*

A shuttle shall be deemed to be of correct pace if, when a player of average strength strikes it with a full underhand stroke from a spot immediately above one back boundary line in a line parallel to the side lines, and at an upward angle, it falls not less than 1 ft., and not more than 2 ft. 6 in. short of the other back boundary line.

Players

5. (*a*) The word 'Player' applies to all those taking part in a game.

(*b*) The game shall be played, in the case of the doubles game, by two players a side, and in the case of the singles game, by one player a side.

(*c*) The side for the time being having the right to serve shall be called the 'In' side, and the opposing side shall be called the 'Out' side.

The Toss

6. Before commencing play the opposing sides shall toss, and the side winning the toss shall have the option of:—

(*a*) Serving first; or

(*b*) Not serving first; or

(*c*) Choosing ends.

The side losing the toss shall then have choice of any alternative remaining.

Scoring

7. (*a*) The doubles and men's singles game consists of 15 or 21 points, as may be arranged. Provided that in a game of 15 points, when the score is 13–all, the side which first reached 13 has the option of 'Setting' the game to 5, and that when the score is 14-all, the side which first reached 14 has the option of 'Setting' the game to 3. After the game has been 'Set' the

score is called 'Love All', and the side which first scores 5 or 3 points, according as the game has been 'Set' at 13- or 14-all, wins the game. In either case the claim to 'Set' the game must be made before the next service is delivered after the score has reached 13-all or 14-all. Provided also that in a game of 21 points the same method of scoring be adopted, substituting 19 and 20 for 13 and 14.

(b) The ladies' singles game consists of 11 points. Provided that when the score is '9-all' the player who first reached 9 has the option of 'Setting' the game to 3, and when the score is '10-all' the player who first reached 10 has the option of 'Setting' the game to 2.

(c) A side rejecting the option of 'Setting' at the first opportunity shall not be thereby barred from 'Setting' if a second opportunity arises.

(d) In handicap games 'Setting' is not permitted.

8. The opposing sides shall contest the best of three games, unless otherwise agreed. The players shall change ends at the commencement of the second game and also of the third game (if any). In the third game the players shall change ends when the leading score reaches:

(a) 8 in a game of 15 points;

(b) 6 in a game of 11 points;

(c) 11 in a game of 21 points;

or, in handicap events, when one of the sides has scored half the total number of points required to win the game (the next highest number being taken in case of fractions). When it has been agreed to play only one game the players shall change ends as provided above for the third game.

If, inadvertently, the players omit to change ends as provided in this Law at the score indicated, the ends shall be changed immediately the mistake is discovered, and the existing score shall stand.

Doubles Play

9. (a) It having been decided which side is to have the first

service, the player in the right-hand service court of that side commences the game by serving to the player in the service court diagonally opposite. If the latter player returns the shuttle before it touches the ground it is to be returned by one of the 'In' side, and then returned by one of the 'Out' side, and so on, until a fault is made or the shuttle ceases to be 'In Play'. (*Vide* paragraph (*b*).) If a fault is made by the 'In' side, its right to continue serving is lost, as only one player on the side beginning a game is entitled to do so (*vide* Law 11), and the opponent in the right-hand service court then becomes the server; but if the service is not returned, or the fault is made by the 'Out' side, the 'In' side scores a point. The 'In' side players then change from one service court to the other, the service now being from the left-hand service court to the player in the service court diagonally opposite. So long as a side remains 'In' service is delivered alternately from each service court into the one diagonally opposite, the change being made by the 'In' side when, and only when, a point is added to its score.

(*b*) The first service of a side in each innings shall be made from the right-hand service court. A 'Service' is delivered as soon as the shuttle is struck by the server's racket. The shuttle is thereafter 'In Play' until it touches the ground, or until a fault or 'Let' occurs, or except as provided in Law 19. After the service is delivered, the server and the player served to may take up any positions they choose on their side of the net, irrespective of any boundary lines.

10. The player served to may alone receive the service, but should the shuttle touch, or be struck by, his partner the 'In' side scores a point. No player may receive two consecutive services in the same game, except as provided in Law 12.

11. Only one player of the side beginning a game shall be entitled to serve in its first innings. In all subsequent innings each partner shall have the right, and they shall serve consecutively. The side winning a game shall always serve first in the next game, but either of the winners may serve and either of the losers may receive the service.

12. If a player serves out of turn, or from the wrong service

court (owing to a mistake as to the service court from which service is at the time being in order), *and his side wins the rally*, it shall be a 'Let', provided that such 'Let' be claimed or allowed before the next succeeding service is delivered.

If a player standing in the wrong service court takes the service, *and his side wins the rally*, it shall be a 'Let', provided that such 'Let' be claimed or allowed before the next succeeding service is delivered.

If in either of the above cases the side at fault *loses the rally*, the mistake shall stand and the players' positions shall not be corrected during the remainder of that game.

Should a player inadvertently change sides when he should not do so, and the mistake not be discovered until after the next succeeding service has been delivered, the mistake shall stand, and a 'Let' cannot be claimed or allowed, and the players' positions shall not be corrected during the remainder of that game.

Singles Play

13. In singles Laws 9 and 12 hold good, except that:—

(*a*) The players shall serve from and receive service in their respective right-hand service courts only when the server's score is 0 or an even number of points in the game, the service being delivered from and received in their respective left-hand service courts when the server's score is an odd number of points.

(*b*) Both players shall change service courts after each point has been scored.

Faults

14. A fault made by a player of the side which is 'In' puts the server out; if made by a player whose side is 'Out', it counts a point to the 'In' side.

It is a fault:—

(*a*) If, in serving, the shuttle at the instant of being struck be higher than the server's waist, or if any part of the head of the racket, at the instant of striking the shuttle, be higher than any part of the server's hand holding the racket.

(b) If, in serving, the shuttle falls into the wrong service court (i.e., into the one not diagonally opposite to the server), or falls short of the short service line, or beyond the long service line, or outside the side boundary lines of the service court into which service is in order.

(c) If the server's feet are not in the service court from which service is at the time being in order, or if the feet of the player receiving the service are not in the service court diagonally opposite until the service is delivered. (*Vide* Law 16.)

(d) If before or during the delivery of the service any player makes preliminary feints or otherwise intentionally baulks his opponent.

(e) If either in service or play, the shuttle falls outside the boundaries of the court, or passes through or under the net, or fails to pass the net, or touches the roof or side walls, or the person or dress of a player. (A shuttle falling on a line shall be deemed to have fallen in the court or service court of which such line is a boundary.)

(f) If the shuttle 'In Play' be struck before it crosses to the striker's side of the net. (The striker may, however, follow the shuttle over the net with his racket in the course of his stroke.)

(g) If, when the shuttle is 'In Play', a player touches the net or its support with racket, person or dress.

(h) If the shuttle be held on the racket (i.e. caught or slung) during the execution of a stroke; or if the shuttle be hit twice in succession by the same player with two strokes; or if the shuttle be hit by a player and his partner successively.

(i) If, in play, a player strikes the shuttle (unless he thereby makes a good return) or is struck by it, whether he is standing within or outside the boundaries of the court.

(j) If a player obstructs an opponent.

(*k*) If Law 16 be transgressed.

General

15. The server may not serve till his opponent is ready, but the opponent shall be deemed to be ready if a return of the service be attempted.

16. The server and the player served to must stand within the limits of their respective courts (as bounded by the short and long service, the centre, and side lines), and some part of both feet of these players must remain in contact with the ground in a stationary position until the service is delivered. A foot on or touching a line in the case of either the server or the receiver shall be held to be outside his service court. (*Vide* Law 14 (*c*).) The respective partners may take up any position, provided they do not unsight or otherwise obstruct an opponent.

17. (*a*) If, in the course of service or rally, the shuttle touches and passes over the net, the stroke is not invalidated thereby. It is a good return if the shuttle having passed outside either post drops on or within the boundary lines of the opposite court. A 'Let' may be given by the umpire for any unforeseen or accidental hindrance.

(*b*) If, in service, or during a rally, a shuttle, *after passing over the net, is caught in or on the net*, it is a 'Let'.

(*c*) If the receiver is faulted for moving before the service is delivered, or for not being within the correct service court, in accordance with Laws 14 (*c*) or 16, and at the same time the server is also faulted for a service infringement, it shall be a let.

(*d*) When a 'Let' occurs, the play since the last service shall not count, and the player who served shall serve again, except when Law 12 is applicable.

18. If the server, in attempting to serve, misses the shuttle, it is not a fault; but if the shuttle be touched by the racket, a service is thereby delivered.

19. If when in play, the shuttle strikes the net and remains suspended there, or strikes the net and falls towards the ground on the striker's side of the net, or hits the ground outside the

court and an opponent then touches the net or shuttle with his racket or person, there is no penalty, as the shuttle is not *then* in play.

20. If a player has a chance of striking the shuttle in a downward direction when quite near the net, his opponent must not put up his racket near the net on the chance of the shuttle rebounding from it. This is obstruction within the meaning of Law 14 (*j*).

A player may, however, hold up his racket to protect his face from being hit if he does not thereby baulk his opponent.

21. It shall be the duty of the umpire to call 'Fault' or 'Let' should either occur, without appeal being made by the players, and to give his decision on any appeal regarding a point in dispute, if made before the next service; and also to appoint linesmen and service judges at his discretion. The umpire's decision shall be final, but he shall uphold the decision of a linesman or service judge. This shall not preclude the umpire also from faulting the server or receiver. Where, however, a referee is appointed, an appeal shall lie to him from the decision of an umpire on questions of law only.

Continuous Play

22. Play shall be continuous from the first service until the match be concluded; except that (*a*) in the International Badminton Championship and in the Ladies' International Badminton Championship there shall be allowed an interval not exceeding five minutes between the second and third games of a match; (*b*) in countries where climatic conditions render it desirable, there shall be allowed, subject to the previously published approval of the National Organization concerned, an interval not exceeding five minutes between the second and third games of a match, in singles or doubles, or both; and (*c*) when necessitated by circumstances not within the control of the players, the umpire may suspend play for such a period as he may consider necessary. If play be suspended the existing score shall stand and play be resumed from that point. Under no

circumstances shall play be suspended to enable a player to recover his strength or wind, or to receive instruction or advice. Except in the case of any interval already provided for above, no player shall be allowed to receive advice during a match or to leave the court until the match be concluded without the umpire's consent. The umpire shall be the sole judge of any suspension of play and he shall have the right to disqualify an offender.

(*The Badminton Association of England has not sanctioned any interval between the second and third games of a match.*)

INTERPRETATIONS

1. Any movement or conduct by the server that has the effect of breaking the continuity of service after the server and receiver have taken their positions to serve and to receive the service is a preliminary feint. (*Vide* Law 14 (*d*).)

2. It is obstruction if a player invades an opponent's court with racket or person in any degree except as permitted in Law 14 (*f*). (*Vide* Law 14 (*j*).)

3. Where necessary on account of the structure of a building, the local Badminton Authority may, subject to the right of veto of its National Organization, make bye-laws dealing with cases in which a shuttle touches an obstruction.

INDEX